Days *of* Deepening Friendship

Other books by Vinita Hampton Wright

Days *of* Deepening Friendship

For the Woman Who Wants Authentic Life with God

VINITA
HAMPTON
WRIGHT

LOYOLA PRESS.
A JESUIT MINISTRY

3441 N. Ashland Avenue
Chicago, Illinois 60657
(800) 621-1008
www.loyolapress.com

Cover design by Kathryn Seckman Kirsch
Interior design by Maggie Hong
Author photo by Jim Wright

Library of Congress Cataloging-in-Publication Data
Wright, Vinita Hampton, 1958–
  Days of deepening friendship : for the woman who wants authentic life
with God / Vinita Hampton Wright.
     p. cm.
  Includes bibliographical references (p.   ).
  ISBN-13: 978-0-8294-2811-7
  ISBN-10: 0-8294-2811-9
  1. Catholic women—Religious life. 2. Spiritual life--Catholic Church. 3.
Friendship—Religious aspects—Catholic Church. I. Title.
  BX2353.W75 2009
  248.8'43—dc22

                                                                2008039971

Printed in the United States of America
08 09 10 11 12 Versa 10 9 8 7 6 5 4 3 2 1

For every woman
whose hunger for love
refuses to die

Contents

PART SEVEN *Engagement*

PART EIGHT *Love*

What can this book do for you?

I have written this book to help women become friends with God.

I say "help" because all one person can ever do for another spiritually is to walk alongside. St. Ignatius of Loyola said it well more than four centuries ago when he reminded spiritual directors to get out of the way and allow the Creator to deal with the created one. He meant that God is already working in people's lives and that their task is to learn how to pay attention to what God is doing. A good spiritual director—or simply a good friend—learns to help a person see more clearly, understand more specifically, and participate more intentionally with God's action in her life.

I say "women" because I have observed for many years how women bring certain qualities to the spiritual life, and how they also face certain challenges. In the Catholic world—and the Christian arena in general—most materials on the spiritual life are still written by men, and their vocabulary and sensibility do not always take into account how women actually experience the world. I am still learning, at age fifty, how my experience as a female has influenced the way I imagine God and relate to God.

This book is not an attempt to re-create the Spiritual Exercises of St. Ignatius, but because Ignatian spirituality makes such effective use of the physical senses, the imagination, and our reflection upon real experience, I have rooted much of this book's material in the Ignatian understanding of spiritual movement. Here is a brief summary of some of the concepts important to the chapters ahead.

We find God in all things. God is ever-present and at work in human experience. We grow by learning to recognize God and respond to God where God already is.

Reflection is a powerful spiritual practice that moves us forward. Reflection involves self-awareness and discernment, combining the ability to understand our interior life with the wisdom to choose our path wisely. We can practice reflection in a number of ways and build into our behavior healthy self-awareness and clarity, leading to good choices.

We are able to know the Divine through a developing friendship with Jesus of Nazareth. As someone "fully human and fully divine," Jesus is able to meet us intimately through reflection, prayer, action, and revelation. In coming to know Jesus, we are able to connect with divine life on a daily basis and in ways that fit our unique situation, personality, and history.

God intends for us to experience inner freedom. This freedom allows us to be who we are rather than try to be someone else. It helps us hold life lightly rather than grasp it anxiously. Spiritual freedom encourages us to receive God's ongoing acceptance, love, and help.

We are designed to participate with God in bringing wisdom and healing to the world through our gifts, desires, and opportunities. Our friendship with God first of all brings healing to us personally; we become increasingly able to deal with our own spiritual conflicts, to offer and seek forgiveness, and to develop and use our particular traits and gifts. As a natural result of our personal healing, we become healers to others, and through our gifts we can't help but do good in the world.

These five points do not offer a comprehensive description of Ignatian spirituality, or even of Christian spirituality. But this book is not meant to be comprehensive. Our main theme is friendship with God. If we apply even one of these concepts with any consistency, the spiritual life will open up, and we will most certainly move forward as people who possess the stunning capacity for authentic life with God.

Experience and belief . . .

The reflections and exercises in this book could be used by women or men. We respond to God first of all as humans, and in Christ "there is no male and female." But I have chosen language and illustrations that focus on women. This is not a book about femininity or feminism but about spiritual movement and how we, as women, interact with divine love.

I have led many writers' workshops, using exercises that helped participants experience the creative process. What I've done here is similar but with a different focus, introducing questions and imaginative exercises designed to help the reader pay closer attention to her life and God's action in it. In these pages I've tried to create an experience, a sequence of chapters and interactions that provide opportunities for spiritual movement and helpful reflection. If the reader does most or all of the exercises, she will truly participate in an unfolding account of her journey with God.

The material is Christian, but I have avoided many religious terms, because often the woman who is ready to delve into a freer and truer friendship with God is in that frame of mind and soul because she has reached a critical point in her life. Many times that critical point comes as the result of suffering, sometimes in church experience or at the hands of religious people. The reader who enters such a season of wanting God's friendship has probably grown weary of the familiar phrases and formulas. This doesn't mean that she no longer believes in God or no longer appreciates church worship and traditional spiritual activities. She may need, however, some distance from a religious experience that has been, or has become, painful or frustrating.

In other words, this material may appeal to someone who is cautious toward traditional religious practice. At the same time, the exercises and reflections will move the reader always toward the heart of authentic belief. I try to help the reader *reconnect* with genuine Christian faith through inviting language and images.

I wrote *Days of Deepening Friendship* with individual readers in mind; it is designed for you to work through on your own. It should work well also with the support of a spiritual director. If you intend to use this book with a small group, please read the suggestions on page 309, "How to use this book with small groups."

Why friendship, and why now?

For many years I have wrestled with belief. I have experienced Christianity with both passion and ambivalence. I have lost faith and found it again, and I have explored more ideas about grace and truth than I can easily remember. But now all I really want is to be God's friend.

I say this without shame: my goal is friendship with the Divine. This is not a new idea. The great Old Testament patriarch Moses was called God's friend, and Jesus called his disciples friends—in fact, he was quite adamant about that distinction. Some of our favorite saints, such as St. Teresa of Ávila and St. Thérèse of Lisieux, included "friend" in their various descriptions of God. I grew up Baptist, without any acquaintance with such saints, but I have considered myself God's friend through the years, even though the concept has grown blurry at times.

But during the past few years, my heart has filled with desire and dissatisfaction, and I'm learning to pay attention to that sort of thing. These symptoms tell me what my soul has known all along: we were made to love God and to increasingly experience God's love for us. If a love relationship with God does not develop, we have missed our purpose, our joy, and our deepest, truest dream.

Now that I am a couple of decades into a career and a marriage, I simply don't have the time and energy I used to have for retreats, seminars, or parish missions. And while I'm not against new information, information does not hold the promise it once did. Especially in this frenetic information age, we are obsessed with data, with acquiring knowledge to catalog and analyze. I still love to learn, but if information does not culminate in friendship with the Divine, I'm not interested.

The deep sense that we need something more . . .

I suspect that whoever has picked up this book feels the same way. After a point, we become weary of thinking so much and trying so hard. We more easily abandon the self-justifying and even the self-helping that in earlier days held such priority for us. Our souls have become needy in a profound, relentless way, and we cannot ignore the symptoms any longer: restlessness, exhaustion, sadness, and fresh desire. These signals tell us that nothing short of divine friendship will do.

If God is not intimate with us, then what's the point of everything else? If God has become mostly a concept or psychological projection—or even a belief system—then we have likely received already whatever benefit can be received from God. I have spent a lifetime conceptualizing God in various ways and projecting my needs and wants onto a divinity that helped me as I chose to be helped. But all of that brings a person only so far.

We become tired of "God" only because much of the time the god we worship is of our own making, a violently skewed version of what the ancients have tried to describe and interpret for us. The prophets and poets, preachers, priests, and popes have brought us to a certain point, but the rest is between us and God Who Is.

Church, Scripture, morality, and what? . . .

I belong to a faith community. I attend church regularly and have for most of my life. I understand that worship helps me and that the Eucharist feeds me; both of these traditional practices place my soul on a track that provides spiritual, psychological, and emotional grounding. Both help me open a little more to who God is and to what God is doing. Because I know this, I have committed myself to a Christian community that honors worship and Eucharist. Still, liturgy is not an end in itself, but a catalyst designed to help us connect to what is mysterious and far beyond our perception. If, somewhere in all the phrases and pauses, the gestures and prayers, God does not reach into my soul and love me, then this spiritual tradition has reached its limits for me.

Sacred texts have always made deep impressions on me. Since childhood I've recognized in Psalms and Gospels matters that my inmost self already knew to be true. I have memorized scores of sacred stories, and they continue to form my interior life and to shape my character in ways that only stories can. And yet, a story—or at least the words that make up a story—bring me to a certain point and no further.

Just think about this. What really fuses a story to a child's heart is not merely the words but the hum of a parent's or grandparent's voice, those tones that vibrate from one body into the other, the warmth of breath against the face, the soft safety of a lap and encircling arms. A story told with love will remain in that child forever. And so, as much as I love Scripture, I will not settle for it cold and cerebral on a page. No, I want God's arms around me while I listen. I want God's breath brushing across the top of my head, and the hum of love moving through me like a song.

Most of us try to live by some sort of moral code. I have to say that the code of Christianity has spared me a lot of pain, has guided me, overall, to healthy decisions and fruitful situations. I don't claim this as any proof of my virtue; my point is that having lived by a proven set of principles has had its advantages. A person really doesn't have to learn everything the hard way.

Even so, it's possible to be moral while frightfully empty. Being a "good person" does not spare us profound depression or dire circumstances. At some point we must ask, Why am I trying to be good? Where does this take me? If all goodness can do is keep life calm—and it doesn't anyway, because life is full of turmoil regardless of my actions—then goodness just isn't good enough.

Does it matter that life is protected by rules for our good if there is no passion flowing through it? Having been a good girl most of my life, I can assure you that being safe is not the same as being fulfilled. It does my soul little good to follow the highest and holiest rules—if God will not befriend me.

Nothing holds still in this universe or stays the same. Everything moves in one direction or another. A life grows better or worse; a relationship evolves or dies. Because movement of some sort will occur, I hope for movement between God and me that brings us closer to life-changing intimacy. And I must suppose that, if God does not intend to terrorize and destroy me, then God has always intended to love me.

Healing our disappointment . . .

I confess that anger resides in my soul, anger rooted in my particular experience of God, or at least in my ideas about how God has dealt with me. I harbor some disappointment in the Divine, and even though I know at an intellectual level that this disappointment probably has more to do with my own perception than with any reality concerning God, I cannot let go of my disappointment simply by deciding to do so. Disappointment and anger go deeper than reason, and they must be healed in that space that is beyond reason.

How many times have I started out not liking a person and then had a complete change of heart as we got to know each other? Friendship takes us past disagreement and disappointment. Friendship helps us receive one another in the spirit of openness. Friendship assumes that we grow into understanding, that in our growing we learn to forgive, and that through our developing relationship we become freer and can allow freedom to each other.

I know that friendship with God lies beyond the definitions of human friendship. But perhaps as I grow in friendship with God, the relationship itself will liberate me from some of my anger and disappointment. If, however, I wait until I no longer "have issues" with God, the potential for friendship might remain stuck in my resentment and hurt.

Stages of relationship . . .

Regardless of our disappointments and various forms of resistance toward God, you and I surely have already enjoyed friendship with the Divine to some extent. But friendship with God, like human relationships, goes through necessary stages—and not all of them feel friendly.

For instance, in the beginning of a marriage, infatuation takes you quite a way, and you are sure that what you're experiencing is fully love. The years show you otherwise; you learn love layer by layer, wound by wound, gift by gift, and revelation by revelation. After years of living with this person, you wake up one day and realize how faulty and frail and self-serving your love truly is. You discover so many falsehoods in yourself that have remained, magically, hidden from yourself.

After a few years of marriage, love no longer connected my husband and me at the surface of life; it submerged us in periods of darkness and confusion out of which we had to feel and fight our way. It wasn't anyone's fault—it was simply the way our love developed in the real world. After a while, though, what I hungered for most was to be the truest, kindest, and most honest friend to this man that it's possible to be. And I wanted him to express to me the truest, deepest friendship possible. He and I have come to understand that if the friendship keeps growing, so many other things heal and get better. The harshest conflicts lose their power when the friendship grabs hold. This intimate, tenacious love makes possible repentance and conversion, and it gives energy to our courage and grace.

The thing to remember is that true friendship culminates from sometimes decades of lesser forms of attachment. Each season of love serves its purpose and moves us toward the more perfect incarnation of divine love. I must remind myself that I have always loved God, however shabbily or stupidly. I was always on the way to loving God better than before. God does not turn away those efforts. God has always been my friend, but such love does its complete work only when it is recognized and welcomed. I hope I'm ready now to welcome that love more intentionally and more bravely.

There will likely always be a place in my life for liturgy and Scripture, for morality and belief—but these things serve, ultimately, the purpose of relationship. Relationship is a living thing, unpredictable and sometimes unnerving, exhilarating and ripe with ecstasies waiting to happen. Perhaps it's the possibility of ecstasy that calls to me now. I've experienced a good enough life, but somewhere along the line I acquired a taste for the *abundant* life. Abundant love—isn't that what we are made for? Can we ever stop desiring it or reaching for it? For today at least, let's dare say to our Creator, "I want to love you, and to be loved by you."

The invitation . . .

I would like you to imagine, now, a room. It is a comfortable room, just the right size and shape, with windows in all the right places, with objects that reassure you and with colors and scents that set you at ease. This is the room you run to for rescue or for rest. This is the room sturdy enough to contain whatever turmoil you must survive and whatever battles you must fight.

And—this is very important—this is a room where lies and fears come to die. This is the room where God dwells, where divine love waits for your arrival. This is the room we will enter now, in order to make friends with God.

Here in the Room

What is your gut reaction to the phrase "friendship with God"?

What have you learned from human relationships that might help you understand relationship with the Divine?

Come up with a phrase or sentence that describes how you feel about this process of deepening your friendship with God.

Write down what you intend to gain from working your way through this book.* Sometimes it helps us grasp an experience when we state a desire or a plan in concrete terms.

---

* It might be helpful to buy a journal to use specifically for working through this book

Part One

Beginning

There is a moment between intending to pray and actually praying that is as dark and silent as any moment in our lives. It is the split second between thinking about prayer and really praying. For some of us, this split second may last for decades. It seems, then, that the greatest obstacle to prayer is the simple matter of beginning, the simple exertion of the will, the starting, the acting, the doing. How easy it is, and yet—between us and the possibility of prayer there seems to be a great gulf fixed: an abyss of our own making that separates us from God.

Emilie Griffin,

Clinging: The Experience of Prayer[1]

When you walk into a room to meet someone, the action is simple enough. But there are layers of feelings, perceptions, memories, assumptions, fears, and desires that come in the door with you. This is why beginning is such a big deal. This is why it can take so long simply to walk through that door.

No matter what state you're in when you enter the Room, it has no impact whatsoever on God's love for you. God's invitation is sweet and clear: Come in! There is so much to know and to experience. And you will be astounded by the divine movement called love.

CHAPTER 1

What has awakened your spiritual desire?

How long must I bear pain in my soul,
and have sorrow in my heart all day long?

Psalm 13:2

On a certain day, during a certain week, something inside you shifts. You feel it happen but aren't really sure what it means. It's as if someone has spoken a little sentence deep in your mind and heart, and once the words are there, you can't ignore them. They tell you what you have needed to know for some time.

What you have discovered is a true desire. It may first appear as merely a need, but those needs that cry out of the deepest part of you are really desires that have been neglected, sometimes for a very long time.

We come to God because we sense a longing so deep we can barely name it. God has planted within us the instinct to cry for help, to seek company, and to name our dreams. We call upon a divine love and power we don't yet understand.

We don't call upon God easily, though. There's nearly always what the novelist or screenplay writer would call an "inciting incident"—something that gives us that initial push.

What has incited you to go on a spiritual search? What motivates you to seek out books on prayer and meditation, or to attend Mass or go to retreats or special events where someone has promised to help you make contact with the Divine? Why, out of all the books available to you, are you reading this one?

What do you need, really? Are you in a stressful situation— critical illness in the family, financial trouble, a rebellious child or estranged spouse, your own unending fatigue or dogged depression? Or do you simply need some room for a dream to grow or for a new plan to form?

Are you on some threshold—about to begin a new job or relationship? Are you pregnant or beginning an adoption process? Are you considering a new career or a geographic move? Perhaps you have come to a stage of life in which you're not sure what is expected of you. Or you are becoming increasingly aware of restlessness in your spirit that is nudging you to a new place.

Which question haunts you when the house becomes too quiet or when you awaken in the middle of the night? Do you wonder if you have made a wrong decision? Are you afraid to die? Are you trying to let go of burdens or take on a new challenge?

Each one of us has interior prompts—signals we experience when we are heading into a crisis or coming to a point when something must change. One of my prompts is fatigue. And if

I go long enough without attending to my fatigue, then fatigue calls in its partner, depression. When I begin to need more sleep than usual, I know that it's time to sit for a while and ask the Holy Spirit to help me put my finger on what the underlying issue is. Am I feeling trapped by an overloaded schedule? Have I become argumentative and ungrateful? Am I worrying about money again?

I've also learned to pay attention to my dreams. They fill up with all sorts of signals that can help me untangle thoughts and emotions. Other prompts are emotional: a sense of urgency, the need for quiet, or a building excitement at the thought of taking a specific step. Sometimes a wonderful revelation will be accompanied by a powerful fit of tears.

The prompts are already there. At some level, you know what you are looking for.

I know it's time for something, maybe not
a profound change but a new way
to consider myself, a better way to walk
through a normal day. It's hard, though,
to hope much or to expect a revelation;
new is not easy for me, especially if it
means imagining myself delightful or
extraordinary, or loved without limit.

Here in the Room

Make a list of your interior prompts. What signals to you that you are moving into crisis mode, or what hints at the unveiling of positive change? Perhaps you have vivid dreams, or you can't sleep. There may be emotional upheaval, such as irritability or weepiness. Some people feel unable to move forward, as if their emotional and mental systems have shut down for a time of rest and repair. Other prompts might be a growing sense of excitement as you approach a positive change, or confirmation in the feedback you get from friends and loved ones. Include in your list anything that could be significant.

Imagine that today you receive a letter in the mail, and the sender of that letter is your own soul. Your deepest self has written to tell you what you need right now and what you should do about it. Write that note now.

For the next few nights, just before you go to bed, review what you have written here in the Room. Allow your own wisdom to mull over these things as you sleep.

CHAPTER 2

How have you managed your life so far?

My wounds grow foul and fester because of my
    foolishness. . . .
I am utterly spent and crushed;
    I groan because of the tumult of my heart.

                                                    Psalm 38:5, 8

Women are the great managers of the universe. Men may do most of the ruling and policing, but if all the women in the world took a nap during the same hour, the earth would probably screech to a halt and bounce right off its axis.

I'm a Boomer woman who was told I could have it all—the career and the babies, the devoted love and the sexual freedom. Thank goodness it took only a few decades to expose such falsehood. Yes, I am capable of doing just about anything. No, I cannot have it all in the same calendar year. Yes, I can live beyond whatever role others may try to carve out for me. No, I cannot be all things to all people. Yes, I can carry enormous burdens when I have to. No, I cannot carry all burdens all the time.

When we decide to accept God's friendship, we must prepare to learn a new way of being in the world. We've grown accustomed to managing life ourselves, even when the constant juggling and burden carrying threaten our health and relationships. If we are going to open our lives to God's love and help, we'll have to clear some space and do some letting go. We may have to come to a complete stop. And, most certainly, we'll need to change the way we cope. Otherwise, this "relationship with God" will become just one more thing to manage.

How do you cope with your life? If you were to receive help from anyone, God included, how would that change the way you go through a day?

It can help, first of all, to look at the containers you use. Everyone has containers—that's where we put the spillover of life. When we are flooded with tasks, responsibilities, emotions, and crises, we have to find something to help us contain it all.

For some of us, the container is *human relationship.* The preferable relationship is a good friend who listens and sits with us patiently without passing judgment or telling us what to do. Friendship can be a wonderful container for the life contents that overflow our personal capacities. We have to learn which friendships can hold up under such responsibility, and we learn eventually how to allow others to help us. A good friend will help carry burdens without absolving us of the responsibility to deal with them. A healthy friend will be a container, but not a personal assistant who encourages us to rely too much on others and not enough on our own developing strength and wisdom.

Because life is not perfect and we aren't either, sometimes the human relationships we choose to help contain life are not well suited to the job. For instance, a new lover might provide relief from the rest of life, but eventually the new wears off and we discover that now we have a whole other set of factors that require good management. This person helped contain some hurt and longing but does not really serve us in the long run. Family members can help contain our spillover to some extent, but even a devoted spouse or parent can't contain our spillover forever. People wear out, no matter how much they love us. Human relationship is not an infallible container.

Other helpful containers might be *fun and adventure, escape and distraction, achievement,* or *helping others.* If we are wise, we know when it's time to take a break, laugh longer and louder than usual, play enthusiastically, or spend a few days doing nothing. We also understand that completing a project or creating something new energizes us to be more hopeful and forward moving. And pouring some of our angst into service for others diverts the overflow while transforming it into more positive energy.

Then again, our favorite containers are not always good for us. For example,

Addiction is a common receptacle for life's overflow. When we are overwhelmed, we drink too much or overeat or work longer hours or go on another shopping spree or obsess over our bodies. We take our stress and trade it in for the momentary relief these things offer. Unfortunately, the source of relief usually ends up adding to our burdens without addressing in any real way what overwhelmed us in the first place.

Rebellion is not really a container, but it can distract us from our real concerns, sometimes for years at a time. We respond to life's overflow by just getting angrier and angrier, and in order to make our anger appear smart and sophisticated, we add a layer of cynicism.

Religious zeal can look like a good container, but if we do not truly get help with our burdens, religion can merely add new ones to the mix. So not only is life too much to handle, but it has now acquired more criteria that make it even more unmanageable. We used to be depressed; now we are depressed and are taking a degree program in theology or pastoral work. Or, still depressed, we are spending weekends trying to help other depressed people at the homeless shelter.

A growing friendship with God will allow some space for reflecting on how we cope with life. Divine wisdom will help us understand which containers we're using, which ones work, and which ones don't.

For example, here are some good options:

Therapy, counseling, or spiritual direction. These are not the same, but they are similar in that they allow another person to help contain what is overflowing in your life. You may benefit from therapy but not spiritual direction, or from spiritual direction but not counseling. When you approach someone for help, it's important to explain what you need, so they can help you determine which sort of help is most appropriate.

A period of rest and retreat. Be careful to choose the right place and time. An expensive vacation in an unfamiliar place can be more stressful than helpful. Time at a religious retreat center can help if you respond well to religious atmosphere. What you may need, however, is a long weekend in bed with some favorite movies—enough of a break to release internal pressure but not long enough to make you feel more behind and overextended.

Tangible help with logistics. If your life is constantly over-whelming, that might be a sign that something has got to go. Relinquish some responsibilities, cut back on social engage-ments, decide that it's probably not wise to go on an extreme diet during the same month you're trying to observe twenty minutes per day of centering prayer. Find a friend or acquaintance who is a good manager and ask for help in reorganizing one or two particularly troubling aspects of your life. Please keep in mind that God did not design you to be self-sufficient. God intends for you to receive help from others sometimes.

As we develop our friendship with God, that place where we meet divine love may well become the ultimate container for all the circumstances, feelings, and situations that are too much for us. And sometimes divine love will direct us to seek a friend, go to counseling, or take longer naps. We can follow through on these directions as our trust grows and as the friendship itself becomes more real to us.

How early did I learn
to hold my life in my own hands?
When did it become sensible, this
fervent self-sufficiency, the refusal to
need anything? And what has it cost me—

in health and in wonder, in lightheartedness
and in gratitude? Can I relinquish
the fear of saying first of all,
"Please" and later, "Thank you"?

Here in the Room

Finish these sentences:

> » The aspects of my life right now that are spilling over are . . .
> » I do have my favorite containers; they are . . .
> » Looking back on my life, I see that how I've often
> coped is . . .
> » It's hard for me to carry every bit of my overwhelming life
> into the Room and give it to divine love because . . .

It might help if you gather some small objects that can represent all the pieces of life you're trying to manage. For instance, a stone can represent financial responsibilities, a little Valentine card can stand in for your relationships, and so on. Find a bowl or a basket that can hold all your objects. Take them out and handle them, allowing yourself to dwell on each one and what it represents to you. Arrange them on a table or the floor, say prayers for each one, and place them back in the bowl or basket. Make a place for this collection where you can get to it easily. This exercise might seem frivolous, but please remember that our five senses are designed to serve us in many ways. Our culture has trained us to approach our problems only through the mind. This exercise allows your physical senses to be part of the process.

CHAPTER 3

What do you expect from this encounter?

To you, O Lord, I call;
my rock, do not refuse to hear me,
for if you are silent to me,
I shall be like those who go down to the Pit.

Psalm 28:1

I grew up under a loving but critical father. I enjoyed his affection and his happiness in being the father of three daughters. But I developed, at an early age, the strong sense that whatever I did would never be quite good enough. Not only that, but most problems I had were in some way my own fault. If something bad happened, then surely I hadn't been careful enough or smart enough or tough enough.

So when at around age ten I discovered within myself a hunger and love for God, I knew that I had a lot of work to do for this relationship to go well. I needed to sharpen my conscience so I wouldn't sin so much. I needed to be good so that God would be pleased with me. My childhood faith sprouted up out of an interesting mixture of Pentecostal, Baptist, and Methodist traditions. Early and often I heard that God forgave us freely, that our ability to have a relationship with God was all because of Jesus' life, death, and resurrection. I knew the Bible verses that attested to these truths.

Nevertheless, the attitude I have most often brought into this friendship with God has been one of shame and disappointment in myself. I know that, hard as I try, the end result is still not good enough. I am not strong enough or dedicated enough or happy enough. God loves me, of course, but it's the kind of love that puts up with people despite the fact that they are screwups. It's still difficult for me to say that God is delighted with me, in the way that any parent is delighted in her child, or in the way I delight in the company of a good friend.

When we enter the Room to befriend God, we bring expectations that are particular to our history and experience. Do we come in confidence of the divine love offered us, or do we drag along an attitude of shame, inadequacy, or something else?

Most of us bring a sense of morality, and this also affects our attitude as we try to make friends with God. Whether I'm aware of it or not, I bring to this meeting my own little system of justice—I come with an idea already in place of what I deserve and don't deserve to get out of this. If I see myself as deficient and unworthy, that perception might effectively block any communication God has for me. It's like a woman who thinks herself ugly, and so even when someone compliments her appearance or tries to flirt with her, she misses the signals entirely. I can miss any signals the Divine sends my way if I've already decided I cannot possibly be the recipient of such grace.

There's a flip side to this personal justice system. If life has been particularly mean to me, or if I have an inflated sense of self-esteem, then I may come into this Room feeling that I am entitled to some form of divine compensation. I come looking for certain blessings and guarantees, and so all I will perceive during this conversation is how God does or does not live up to those expectations. I will not hear God very well because I filter out everything but the words I want to hear. Many of us fail to hear God's voice because it does not speak to us on our own terms.

How I have experienced love shapes my expectations of God, who is supposed to love me. What this means in very practical terms is that I bring into this Room my failed romances, the lost opportunities for love. I bring the vacant place in my soul where I had hoped a marriage would reside. Or I bring the jagged missing piece known as the marriage that failed. I bring into this Room my present significant relationship, whether it is thriving or crippled.

My experience as a woman may condition me to expect that God is always ready with new demands for my time and energy. I may therefore come to the encounter desperate to be left alone. I am tired of preparing meals, solving problems, serving on committees, and monitoring the well-being of friends, children, and pets. I'm tired of tidying up and sorting out. I'm tired of getting organized and giving sex. When I enter the Room where I imagine God is waiting, I bring the nagging fear that God is going to present yet another task to add to my list. These sorts of expectations do not enhance my approach to divine friendship.

If, in my history of girlhood and womanhood, there reside trauma and violence, I come to this meeting place on high alert. If I have been conditioned to think of God as exclusively male, or even primarily male, there is no way this meeting begins comfortably for me. I come expecting that I must somehow protect myself, wanting a buffer against any other presence, divine or not. I arrive with memories that will not stay silent, and with a weak hope that God will not touch me without my permission. Perhaps I have read the lengthy history of God's interaction with the people of Israel, and I know that at times God put them where they didn't want to be and allowed them to suffer what they wished to avoid. These thoughts do not encourage me to approach God now. For all women who carry in themselves a history of violation, the Magnificat has never made a lot of sense. We cannot say happily, with Mary the undefiled maiden, "Do with me whatever you will." We wonder if her response would have been the same if she had suffered as we have.

So for us, there must be different Scripture, at least in the beginning. If we are fortunate, we have also read the words of the prophet Hosea, who speaks in God's voice when he says, "I will bring you to a quiet place and speak tenderly to you." Because of my great damage, I can approach God only if God is willing to wait and to woo, to give me the time I need and to hold back power until I can understand that this is power I share.

When we approach relationship with God, it's important to understand what our true expectations are. We must consider expectations we have of ourselves, and expectations we have of

God. Sometimes, if we dig a little, we'll begin to understand what is behind our fear, doubt, or hesitation.

Please, oh please
let me sit here awhile and just be calm,
be okay, be myself not needing
so many excuses.
Is it really acceptable in your sight
that I haven't loved very well, and that
I get tired so easily?
It will be really nice if, first of all,
we don't make any lists.

Here in the Room

Try to describe your personal system of justice—the moral judgments and problems you bring into this encounter with God.

How does your history of love relationships affect how you approach relationship with the Divine?

Imagine God as a physical person who is sitting in the Room when you enter. When God first sees you, what look comes across his or her face? What expression is there, and how does it make you feel? When God greets you, what are the words, and what is the tone of voice? Does God rise and come to meet you? Does God embrace you or grip your hand with enthusiasm, or is there another response?

How do you feel once you're here in the Room with God? What are your fears and doubts? What do you hope for?

When you first speak to God, what words come out of your mouth?

CHAPTER 4

Where have you come from?

My frame was not hidden from you,
when I was being made in secret,
intricately woven in the depths of the earth.
Your eyes beheld my unformed substance.
In your book were written
all the days that were formed for me,
when none of them as yet existed.

Psalm 139:15–16

When we set out on a spiritual journey, we begin at a place specific to us. We might liken life to an immense, endless river, and each of us steps into that river from our own place on the bank. Some of us are fortunate enough to wade in where the current kisses our ankles and the sandy bank gradually takes us to deeper, faster waters. Our birth is a happy occasion, surrounded by a loving family and the advantages of material abundance. Yet, while we are easing out to the middle of swirling adulthood, some of our contemporaries, born into poverty and broken family systems, are being tossed over cliffs into the rapids, barely making it into the river alive. Or perhaps we are the ones with rocky beginnings, having entered life's river from a dangerous or ugly place.

I stepped into the river from a region of the Bible Belt in southeast Kansas. It was a gentle enough beginning, a childhood developing within the homey confines of rural churches, simple pleasures, and extended family. We looked and acted like just about everyone else in that small community, which meant that we were used to certain emotional comforts and were also conditioned early to conform to what was "normal." Our part of the riverbank was wide and choked with grasses; a person had to wade seemingly forever to find anything more exciting than a few fish.

Because my stepping-off point was so saturated with a form of Christian religion, I actually had to leave faith for a time in order to come at it afresh as an adult. This is not an unusual sequence for many of us who were brought up in a religious setting. Because the atmosphere of belief and ritual becomes so familiar, we mistakenly think that we know what faith is—we even think we know what God is like. Sooner or later, the familiar isn't good enough; we come to a dead end and discover that the true Divine is a stranger to us. We begin to understand that knowing about God—through what we learned from Sunday school or catechism—is not really the same as knowing God.

For the woman who did not grow up surrounded by religion, entering a friendship with God might be completely different. As a youngster or an adult, she is attracted to faith for a certain reason. Perhaps, like Dorothy Day, her passion for social justice causes her to bump right into Jesus Christ. Or, like Anne Lamott, the strange, impossible love and acceptance of other Christians toward her—a drug user, cynic, and struggling single mom—simply overwhelms her and changes life forever.

The point is, when we embark upon any pilgrimage of the soul, such as friendship with God, it is important to understand where we come from. Our spiritual needs in the present will be shaped by our religious experiences of the past. I can't count how many people I've met who were raised Catholic and journeyed into an evangelical Protestant faith as adults, or who were raised Baptist and had become practicing Catholics by the time they were thirty. This movement from one tradition to another—or even from one religion to another—rarely represents defiance. Rather, it represents our need to come to faith as adults, and often this involves breaking away from childhood practices long enough to assess our beliefs in a colder, clearer light.

Sometimes we discover that we have been rejecting the faith of our childhood not based upon the faith itself but in reaction to other things that were attached to it. Because so many of the Christians I knew growing up seemed afraid of intellectual pursuit, or were in some cases blatantly anti-intellectual, I was tempted to abandon Christianity in order to do well in college and expand my intellectual horizons. Other people need to put distance between themselves and a hierarchical church system that has caused much damage to people they loved. Some of us associate faith with passivity, having known too many religious people who seemed to sit around waiting for God to solve their problems. Others of us cannot open a Bible or kneel to pray without recalling authority figures such as parents, priests, or teachers who quoted the Bible and were outwardly pious, yet treated others with cruelty and suspicion.

It's not just our religious history that influences our present movement toward God. Our beginning in life—that part of the riverbank from which we started—taught us all sorts of lessons about who we were and what kind of a world we lived in.

I used to wonder why holidays
were so much better when I was a kid.
All that food, rooms filled with grown-ups
who told stories and laughed a lot.
I remember certainty and comfort.
But there were also the divorces and
family squabbles, the layoffs and
lingering illnesses, the daily
hardness of everything. My happiness
was real, but theirs was embellished
for my sake, I think.
They didn't really lie, just didn't
tell me everything.
I have carried that silence for decades,
am finally deciphering the hurtful
words and anguished pauses,
am unwrapping the gifts

shuttled into drawers and corners
that no one back then could open.

––––––––––––––– ▬ –––––––––––––––

Here in the Room

Describe the beginning of your life in terms of a river. If you like, choose one or more of the adjectives below.

» peaceful

» turbulent

» meandering

» rushing

» dangerous

» stagnant

» teeming

» polluted

» clear

» playful

» refreshing

Write down some of the things older family members or friends have mentioned about that time. Are there significant stories surrounding your birth or that particular era in the family's history?

Which people made up your family back then, when you were a child? Make a list, and beside each name, write one short statement that, for you, describes that person's presence in your life.

Respond to whichever of these statements most applies to you.

» Ours was a fairly typical nuclear family: parents and kids, with at least one grandparent in regular contact. If I could describe my family with a phrase it would be:

» Ours was, in my view, a remarkable family, and here's why:

» Ours was not a typical family, for these reasons:

» Ours was a damaged and dysfunctional family, although I understand now that some love did exist. The phrase I would use to describe my family is:

Which of these statements rings true for you?

» My birth was anticipated and welcomed with much joy.

» My birth was accepted and adjusted to. I'm sure my parents were happy at my birth, but I've always felt I disrupted their lives by getting born.

» My birth was cause for much stress in our family, and here's why:

Beyond your immediate family, what was your community like during childhood? List the people, organizations, groups, and institutions you would consider significant influences upon your growing-up years. Beside each name, write two or three adjectives that best describe what that person or group meant to you.

Which of these statements rings most true for you?

» My childhood neighborhood was a great place to grow up.

» My childhood neighborhood was a dump, and I couldn't wait to get out of there.

» My childhood neighborhood was filled with mostly decent people, but as an adult I can look back and recognize these common unhealthy patterns or ideas:

» We moved so much when I was a kid that I don't connect my history with any one place very well.

CHAPTER 5

Who, and what, comes with you?

He established a decree in Jacob,
and appointed a law in Israel,
which he commanded our ancestors
to teach to their children;
that the next generation might know them,
the children yet unborn,
and rise up and tell them to their children,
so that they should set their hope in God . . .

Psalm 78:5–7

Not only do we enter the river from a certain place, determined by who our family is and where we come from, but we embark upon our journey carrying bags we did not pack ourselves.

When I waded into the life of faith, I hauled along suitcases full of presumptions, stories, beliefs, and memories handed down by relatives, pastors, church members, and schoolteachers. The faith community dominating our small town propagated a specific kind of Jesus and quite certain ideas about God and heaven, sin and redemption, morality and grace.

Our god was a rather judgmental man who was impossible to please and who would figure out what I most wanted to do and then pick its polar opposite as my destiny. That god hated homosexuals, atheists, secular humanists, and women who had abortions. That god loved America in a special way and was quoted most accurately in the King James version of the Bible. That god became nervous and indignant when I asked too many questions. And, although I never would have voiced such statements back then, it seemed to me that the god of my town was easily threatened by girls like me who were intelligent and had dreams of our own.

Before I knew it, I was a young woman professing to believe a lot of things I had merely been taught but had never really learned for myself.

Which isn't to say that all my inherited baggage was harmful or useless. Some items packed by loved ones and other significant people remain to this day my cherished possessions. A faith tradition is important for many reasons, one of them our need to be formed spiritually from childhood. But we always end up with stuff that must be tossed away as the years go by. Some of it is extra stuff, and some of it is toxic stuff. We can only sort it out as we go.

It's important that we unpack the bags that others have packed for us, look carefully at each item, and decide what to do with it. Some of us decide to carry along quite a few of those original items, such as our belief in one God who is over all, or our trust in a process called prayer, or our confidence in a set of principles, such as the Ten Commandments or the Beatitudes. Some others of us must leave behind—or discard along the way—all the items in our bags. Sometimes we discard these things more because of their association with people and experiences than because of what we think of the items themselves.

Not only do we drag along items in bags we did not pack, but we also bring with us past relationships. Each of us is raised in a family of one sort or another, even if that family turns out to be foster care or a convergence of two or more families. And with every relationship comes a combination of conflict and nurture. Whatever battles we have waged with the significant people in our lives, we will repeat those battles to some degree as we try to be in relationship with new people. We will even repeat those battles as we try to be in relationship with God.

Past relationships therefore matter a lot. When we decide to approach the Divine, we engage first in the same ways we have engaged with other people. Our relational history determines what we bring to our spirituality.

Just think about how you approach new relationships. Are you able to be open fairly quickly, or do you usually feel the need to hold back information or hold back your emotional response, your commitment, or other aspects of yourself?

Do you generally trust people, or is your first response some form of fear or suspicion?

When you enter a relationship, does it feel like a happy exploration, or are you on the lookout for danger? Perhaps you're inclined to be cautious, even to the point of calculating what you will give to this relationship and when.

I have always been slow to open up to people. Also, I tend not to go into relationships expecting them to be huge resources for me. These attitudes are due in part to an introverted nature. But they developed in a family system that was fairly closed to outsiders and that put a high value on a person solving her own problems and being self-sufficient generally. For many years, I saw friendship as something to enjoy but not to need. It only followed that I've tended to feel a bit guilty for needing God; my inclination is to feel that I should have been able to manage all right without help, that I had failed God by not being better at life.

From my starting place—my bend in the river—I learned that I must always be nice and polite and do what I was told. I learned to distrust my deepest desires and most honest assessments—if they digressed from conventional wisdom. I learned to avoid conflict and to reject unattractive emotions such as anger and grief, and to dismiss out of hand spiritual responses such as despair and doubt. There are many other things I absorbed there at the beginning place of my life, but you get the idea.

By now you are probably thinking back to your own beginning place and to the sort of work it did on your soul, which should lead naturally to the work you must now do.

I remember visiting a friend of Grandma's
who, on that July day,
gave me a Fudgesicle. I knew
right away she was good people,
to be trusted. The same with
the old German woman who,
chattering happy syllables,
tossed oranges over the hedge for us kids.
But then Uncle George picked up
my pet rabbit by the ears,
and I thought of him differently after that.
Also, that pastor was unkind to my sister,
my math phobia began with
Mrs. Green in eighth grade, and I hated
how weak my mother seemed
in the face of Dad's dark moods.
I've tried to leave behind the
uncomfortable parts,
but some days I run into every person
who ever hurt me.

Here in the Room ☕____

Consider the major relationships that influenced you early in life, in the way you related to others and to God. Finish the statements that apply to you. If you like, add a few lines about the people you identify.

>> The person(s) who nurtured me and kept me safe was/ were:

>> The person(s) whom I associated with punishment and fear was/were:

>> The person(s) I turned to for assistance or for wisdom was/were:

>> The person(s) I trusted with my secrets was/were:

>> The person(s) I sought out for fun and good company was/were:

>> The person(s) who most contributed to my spiritual progress was/were:

>> The person(s) who most hindered and harmed my spiritual progress was/were:

>> The person(s) with whom I experienced the most consistent conflict was/were:

A little story . . .

I first remember talking with another person about God / spiritual matters when I was age _____. This conversation came about because _____. The way I felt emotionally during this conversation could best be described as _____. My response to the other person was, for the most part, [positive / negative]. If I

learned anything from that discussion, it would be this: _____.
As I look back on that encounter, I can see that it contributed [a
lot / a little] to my perceptions and beliefs about _____.

What's in your bag . . .

Try to list some of the things that others packed for you.

» These are attitudes and habits used to create comfort or
  safety:

  examples: Don't trust outsiders. Do trust those in authority.

» These are specific beliefs—about faith, prayer, work,
  guilt, and so forth:

  *examples: People are basically sinful / okay. I will be rewarded
  if I work hard.*

» These are skills and gifts passed along to me:

  *examples: Skill at stretching a buck. Gift of soothing others'
  hurt feelings.*

» These are prejudices and fears passed along to me:

  *example: People who don't believe in God are morally inferior
  to those who do, and it's best if we don't associate with them
  too much.*

Remember, you are here in the Room with God. And
although you may have made some discoveries while doing
these exercises, nothing you've written down is a surprise to the
Divine. Spread out what you've written and ask for the grace to
see your life clearly.

Dwell a little longer . . .

At this point, you may have generated quite a bit of material from the Here in the Room sections of the book. It's possible that memories have been coaxed out of hiding, making this experience somewhat emotional. If so, try to allow yourself to dwell awhile with all that memory and emotion. Place your written responses on a table, or spread them out on your bed or the floor. Or sit in a comfortable chair with this book or your journal on your lap.

Remember now that you and your responses are in the Room. You have brought yourself and your memories to sit here in God's presence, because you need support as you take in so many important aspects of your history.

And remember, this Room is a safe place. It can hold your life story in endless wisdom. In this Room, you can allow profound peace to surround you because this is not a Room for judgment. No one is going to say to you, "How could you have been so stupid, or mean, or misled?" Divine love is not the least interested in success or failure but only in the reality you have experienced and carried with you.

Do not try to fix anything—history is history, and there's nothing for you to fix. Don't worry over what should have happened. Don't apologize to yourself or to anyone else for how this history has gone or how you participated in it. (In a few more chapters, we will deal with resistance and confession; now is not the time.) All you are to do is sit with your history—with the situations and people who formed you—and let it be.

If you would like to be a little daring . . .

Simply rest your arms in your lap or raise them slightly. Then turn your palms upward and open them. This sounds simple, but it is a physical gesture that expresses your soul opening and your heart letting go. The situations and communities that birthed you, and the people who influenced you so dramatically for good or for ill—you are, in a small, beginning sort of way, releasing them from your grasp. You are handing over this history to God's embrace and safekeeping.

Don't worry if you can't forgive all the hurts or figure out all the mistakes; these are not your tasks for now. At this moment you are in this Room with God, and you are offering to God this portion of trust, just enough faith to loosen your grip and unload some burden. That's all.

Help along the way . . .

You may or may not want to try this final thing; feel free as you are able. Take up your journal or sketchpad, and listen for anything God might say to you today in this Room. It's possible that you'll begin writing or drawing immediately, spilling out the very words or images your soul needs.

How will you know if these messages come from God? After all, we're inclined to interpret things in our own skewed ways. We also tend to think we're hearing God when we're really listening to echoes of statements pressed upon us by others or by our own desperate needs and fears. It's not always a simple thing to hear what God is saying—so many things can get in the way.

There are, though, a few guidelines to discerning God's voice. We will certainly learn more as we spend time in this Room and on this journey. For now, consider:

God's words have the ring of truth. When we hear them—whether within ourselves or from other people—our soul resonates deeply, sometimes even before our reason takes hold of the words. Even if we don't fully understand what we're hearing, we know it is true, and for that reason we are compelled to pay attention.

God's words are given for our healing and spiritual progress. They do not beat us down or fill us with depression and regret. Sometimes when we hear God, our initial response is sorrow over our own mistakes and resistance, but underneath our reaction flows a sense of hope. Divine communication *encourages* our inmost being. Even when God reveals something negative that must be dealt with, that wisdom is accompanied by compassion.

Sometimes God speaks to us through and with another person. If your soul is too wounded and weary to continue this journey alone, you may experience God in the words and presence of a pastor, friend, counselor, or spiritual director. Don't hesitate to seek a companion if stress, pain, exhaustion, or depression consistently hinders your steps.

It may help to think about what kind of experience you have had with the material in these chapters. Feel free to write about it now. Or express your reaction through drawing, singing, or whatever is natural and helpful.

If you like, write a brief response to God. Call it a prayer or just a little statement that sums up your response to this bit of time in the Room.

PART TWO

Hesitation

Avoid being bashful with God, as some people are, in the belief that they are being humble. It would not be humility on your part if the King were to do you a favor and you refused to accept it; but you would be showing humility by taking it, and being pleased with it, yet realizing how far you are from deserving it. A fine humility it would be if I had the Emperor of heaven and earth in my house, coming to do me a favor and to delight in my company, and I were so humble that I would not answer his questions, nor remain with him, nor accept what he gave me, but left him alone. . . . Have nothing to do with that kind of humility, but speak with him as with a father, a brother, a Lord and a spouse—and, sometimes in one way and sometimes in another, he will teach you what you must do to please him. Do not be foolish; ask him to let you speak to him.

St. Teresa of Ávila,

The Way of Perfection[2]

If you're like most people, your movement toward God is not smooth, immediate, or in a straight line. Things keep getting in the way, some of them on the road itself and some within you. Sometimes before you can move forward you must figure out what causes the hesitation in your steps.

You may have been desperately wounded, or you may have enjoyed a life quite free of turmoil. Whatever your history, you are in this Room right now with God. Not you and the rest of the human race. Not you and all other women. Not even you and Eve or the Virgin Mary. You face this opportunity as the one soul you are.

So, what is stopping you—or, as St. Teresa might put it, why are you being so bashful?

CHAPTER 6

How do you approach God of the universe?

> When I look at your heavens, the work of
>   your fingers,
>   the moon and the stars that you have
>   established;
> what are human beings that you are
>   mindful of them,
>   mortals that you care for them?
>
> Psalm 8:3–5

From the time St. Thérèse of Lisieux was a little girl, she enjoyed a free and loving relationship with her father, Louis Martin. She did not fear him, but trusted him, adored him, and enjoyed his respect. Louis's regard for his young daughter was such that, when at age fourteen she told him she wanted to follow her two older sisters to the Carmelite convent, he gave his permission, although it broke his heart to lose one more daughter to a cloistered life. Louis supported Thérèse's desire by speaking on her behalf with the mother superior (because Thérèse was too young by several years to join the convent), by taking her to see the bishop, and finally by accompanying her to an audience with the pope.

This affectionate relationship with her father no doubt prepared Thérèse to give herself wholeheartedly to God the Father and to take permanent vows as a bride of Jesus Christ. For her, loving God was an open and passionate expression of herself to a divine presence she trusted and clung to even when she wasn't happy about the way "he" sometimes treated her. Thérèse's approach to life with God was so fresh and authentic that, despite her lack of higher education and her early death at age twenty-four, she was made a saint in 1925 and declared a Doctor of the Church in 1997. Although Thérèse was obedient and dedicated in her life as a nun, there are various hints that she longed for every gift in the Christian life, including that of serving as a priest—womanhood posed obstacles even for her. Nevertheless, she felt a strong calling to support the work of the clergy and counseled two priests through extensive correspondence nearly up until her death.

For Thérèse, approaching God was not hindered by her social place as a woman in nineteenth-century France or by her perception of God as Father and Husband. But each of us must ask ourselves: What does it mean that I—a woman in this place and time—am trying to relate to God?

Many of us who are much over the age of thirty come to this encounter perceiving God not that differently from how Thérèse did—as a powerful male sort of deity. If this is your approach, then you likely see yourself (subconsciously at least) as a female who must attract God's attention or get his approval. Depending on what your life with men has been like, you will think of God as welcoming or harsh, accepting or judgmental. You may have enjoyed various healthy relationships with men. If so, then even if you think of God as male-like, you are able to welcome God freely as a divine version of father or lover or brother or friend.

Maybe you have developed a concept of the Divine as more feminine than masculine. You sense first of all the motherly nurture of God's love—alluded to various times in Scripture and in the writings of saints—and the close companionship of someone who walks alongside you as a sister would. This motherly or sisterly sense of God makes it easier for you to open up without qualm to the wisdom of God the mentor and companion. But there can be just as many problems with seeing God as mainly female as in seeing God as mainly male. Your female relationships (with mother, sisters, teachers, supervisors, and so on) also influence what you think is required of you when approaching God's presence. We don't solve our "god issues" simply by shifting the divine gender!

We know, intellectually at least, that God transcends our sensibilities and is not defined by gender at all. The issue isn't whether to call God "Father" or something else. When it comes to approaching God, seeking to have a relationship that is meaningful to us, we must take into account our automatic assumptions and our emotional habits.

Perhaps you come to God with a strong sense of your own power to create, that physical ability to be a home for new life and growth. Many people feel closer to God after they become parents. They now experience the sort of love Jesus was hinting at when he called God "Father." If this is true for you, then you might feel a true partnership with God, and you believe at a deep level that you are honorable in God's sight.

If sexuality has been a prominent theme in your life, you might approach the Divine with much passion. Loving God has elements of fun and abandon. The woman who can approach God in this way enjoys merging her religious beliefs with physical, earthy reality. This sort of woman can easily see the ordinary details of her life as sacramental, as having a deeper meaning.

Your most impressive experiences of the Divine might have grown out of community. For you, the face of God is the face of people who have loved and helped you, and whom you have loved and helped. You feel God's presence as you worship with others and as you try to work with others to do good things in the world. Or perhaps you come in and extend your hand to God in friendship, but in all honesty you expect that God is sizing you up, judging your imperfections so that you can work on them later.

Some of us know divine presence mostly through the intuition with which women often are so well-equipped. You may not possess a lot of religious education or training, but you certainly know when you have heard God's voice or felt God's presence. Your experience of the Divine is more likely to be outside church settings, and it is attached to your own deep wisdom.

One way or another, we bring our body-ness to God. A woman's body has strong agendas of its own, a seemingly wild chemistry that can make a person feel that she is never truly in charge of her days and hours. If we are fortunate, we learn how to listen to this body, how to attend to it with love and wisdom. For many of us, though, our body represents more battle than not. The prevailing culture never prepared us to commune with our physical selves, and the medical industry has taught us to see the female body more or less as a machine with numerous capacities for malfunction. Some of us what if i spend a large portion of our time trying to fix our bodies, to make them behave, to change their appearance and performance. Some of us even learn early to hate who we are physically.

Our creativity, our passion, our relationships, our intuition, our hate or ambivalence or frustration—we bring it all into the Room. Even as we kneel to pray or close our eyes or find a comfortable position for sitting while we meditate and try to converse with God, we come in this physical body, and all that we think and feel about our body is right here with us as we try to connect with the Divine.

Whatever your usual approach to God, please understand that it might be an effective way for you to connect—and it might not. In fact, our well-worn perceptions often get in the way of our being open and trusting in divine friendship. Are you willing to examine your perceptions of this encounter?

———————————————

God of Everything,
Your eyes remind me of someone
who adored me once, back when
love was easier to accept.
Some days I can bear your gaze

without finding some busy thing to do.
In my kinder moments I imagine
that you sit, all beautiful and friendly,
listening to each word I say, as though
my thoughts are fully formed and
I know things that matter.

Here in the Room

Have you perceived the Divine as mainly one gender or another? If so, how has that affected the way you approach friendship with God?

Try to invent a perception of God that is quite different from what has been the usual one for you. For instance, if God is usually a white male, change that image to an African woman. If God has been too American, change God into a Pakistani or a Portuguese. Try to spend some time communicating with this fresh vision of the Divine.

How have your religious experiences, if any, influenced the way you thought of God, or the way you felt you were *supposed* to think of God?

If you had to describe God to your young daughter, what would you say?

CHAPTER 7

What do you bring to this friendship?

Because your steadfast love is better than life,
my lips will praise you.
So I will bless you as long as I live;
I will lift up my hands and call on
your name.

Psalm 63:3–4

In the movie *Marvin's Room*, we meet Bessie, who has spent her adult life in the family home caring for her father who, she says jokingly to her doctor, "has been dying for twenty years." Bessie's doctor discovers that she has leukemia, and so Bessie must contact her estranged sister, Lee, and Lee's sons so that they can be tested for compatibility as potential bone marrow donors. Lee ran away from family responsibility years ago, and it's clear that she thinks Bessie has thrown away her life by never marrying and tending their bedridden father and their senile Aunt Ruth.

In one of the final scenes, Bessie's doctor calls to tell her that none of her relatives is a match; there will be no bone marrow transplant. After she tells Lee, the two of them hug and then continue sorting their father's many medications. Suddenly Bessie says passionately how lucky she is to have had her father and aunt to care for, to have had so much love in her life. Lee says that she's sure their father and Aunt Ruth love Bessie very much. But Bessie says no, that's not what she meant. The love she referred to was what she was able to give. "I've been so lucky to have been able to love someone so much!"

Here is a woman who was more attentive to what she brought to a relationship than what she got from it. In the midst of a life that many people would see as limited, Bessie had grown to appreciate who she was and what she was capable of giving.

If we expect to become friends with God, we must believe that we have something to offer. The history of God's relationship with the people of Israel is a long story of God's saying, in essence, "I have all of this love for you! Why don't you respond? Bring yourself to me; offer your gifts to this friendship. I am waiting for you to talk to me, to tell me your troubles, to dwell with me." Today still, divine love longs for reciprocity. You and I have something to offer God.

To be honest, some days when I approach something like prayer, sending words and thoughts and gestures into outer space, I feel a little silly. I mean, really, does the fact that I have recited the Lord's Prayer mean anything at all? Does it matter that I have just said to the window that faces my back yard, "God, I offer myself to you today—help me walk with wisdom and love"?

And even if I believe that divine love is eager for friendship with me, how do I participate if I don't have a sense of what I bring to this encounter? I have to consider who I am to be offering my presence to anyone, let alone to God. To take it a step further, I must consider what my womanhood adds to this mix, because I am fitted in particular ways to express friendship, thanks to my history, experience, and unique place in the world.

I am a woman of a certain race and age. I cannot separate these characteristics from the rest of me; I cannot come to God merely as a free-floating soul that arrives from nowhere and belongs nowhere. I come with an identity, not one I chose but one I possessed at birth and have developed since then. My spiritual life is not spiritual only; my soul is one with this identifiable body.

I am a woman who has helped other women bear their burdens, whether wayward children or cancerous growths. The community of womanhood has formed on its own; I didn't really seek it. It is mine because of my gender. I know, in a far-reaching way, the many forms of happiness and tragedy that visit women everywhere. I cannot help but know these things. They shape my thinking and my feeling. My experience of other women arranges a sort of prejudice in my system, affecting the way I see life, and it develops sensitivities I would not otherwise possess.

I am a woman who has longed for passionate love. I know what real longing is because I have endured it time and again. I know that romantic, sexual longing is a whisper of human longing for divine embrace. I know that such longing can consume everything in its path, that it is exquisitely beautiful but because of its tremendous power can bring danger with it.

I am a woman who has enjoyed relationships with men but who has also been hurt by men. My experience with the opposite sex has given me biases and sensitivities that I cannot help bringing to my encounter with God.

I am a woman who has learned the value of waiting, of pondering much in my heart before taking action or speaking out. My own body—through pregnancy, cycles, and seasons—teaches me that life has a way of ripening in its own time, and that good things rarely happen quickly or appear instantly.

I am the daughter of a mother, the granddaughter of grandmothers. I am sister and aunt and wife and mother. I am friend and mentor. I am nearly always aware that the web of life is expansive and that my time and space in it are precious yet short-lived.

What do I bring to this hoped-for friendship with God besides my person? What gifts come with me when I enter the Room?

I bring love, which I'm good at, having practiced it since childhood. The kind of devotion I first lavished on pets and play-mates is well developed now for greater challenges.

I bring attentiveness. Because I have managed a household and held down various jobs, I can focus on a task or a person with chaos going on all around me.

I bring an active, seeking mind. I learn fast simply because life demands it.

I bring many talents. Some of them, yet undiscovered, are waiting for their time.

I bring a willingness to dream bigger and hope more. Sometimes no one else will. I have ample experience in taking up the slack when others don't come through.

I bring honesty and a lack of pretense. There is no space in my life for nonsense.

When, in hope of forming a relationship, I come into the place where I will meet God, *I bring what my mother gave me, what grandmothers and aunts gave me*—all the stories of being female in this world, all the tears and belly laughter, the gutsiness along with the grace. I come equipped with breasts and ovaries—or with some grief over their loss—and with sexual hunger and its natural rising and falling, its tension and release.

I come also with my deep instinct to birth and to nurture, whether I have many children or remain childless. I bring to God the severe pain of barrenness or the severe pain of mothering a lost or suffering child. I bring my enormous capacity to hold the lives of others, because women are born with the ability to be wombs for the human race. In us reside the poetry and songs of suffering and endurance. We hold memory as sacred and necessary and so tell the stories from one generation to the next. We take in the stray animals and sometimes the wandering adults. We literally carry life within us. We carry life in many other ways as well.

And, finally, when I approach God in friendship, *I bring the faith that never got written down.* Although today women may be well-educated and articulate, we have been formed by many prior generations of women who could not read or write— women who did not contribute in a tangible, provable way to the composing and compiling of sacred Scripture. Of course I can claim Scripture as part of my spiritual heritage. I can see it as my sustenance and revere it as the divine communication it is. But any religion that is Scripture-based is not immediately the property of women. We bore no influence upon the writing, the scholarship, the early discussions about what got included and what was left out. Many of our own stories did not make the final cut. The Bible, or the Torah, or the Koran, never belonged to us, in the same way that they did not belong to the poor, the uneducated, and the marginalized.

Faith, however, has always remained with us. And divine communication was never limited to written-down words. *Women have always been the bearers of the unwritten-down.* We developed other aspects of religion, those not so tied to phrase and document. Ours was the other side of faith—the story-keeping and the prayer that are the natural result of intuition. Ours was the wisdom that shouted loudly in God's created world and that came to us in dream. God does not require books. The Holy still speaks to people who have no books and no education. The Spirit still thrives in those who, because of those deficiencies, have little or no power in this life.

So when we come to God, we can bring the Scripture but a lot of other things besides. The Divine is well acquainted with our unwritten-down faith. In fact, the Spirit often relies on women to help the rest of humanity learn again to dream and to welcome visions.

I inherited my grandmother's china
cabinet. Many old dishes wink behind
the curved glass, very pretty and delicate,
harboring stories. The rose tea set
was Great-Grandma's wedding gift.
Some time ago I filled the sugar bowl,
then returned it to the oak shelf after
the tea was drunk. Every now and then,
when dusting, I lift the lid, see the sugar
still there and think about sweetness,
good things contained within a life,
maybe for decades, waiting for a certain
day, or the next guest—it is
the always present quality in the room.

Here in the Room ☕

I hope that, by now, you have begun to think about who you are and what you bring into the Room where you become friends with God. Here are some questions to help along those thoughts.

Try to look at yourself as an outside observer might. What do you look like? What is your age, your ethnic background, your current situation in life? What character traits of yours become apparent after half an hour of casual conversation?

Describe yourself as your mother would describe you. Even if your mother is not living or has never been very involved with you, try to see yourself from a mother's viewpoint, including not merely physical attributes but personality traits as well.

Describe yourself as your grandmother would describe you.

Choose two men you know fairly well, and try to describe yourself as they might see you.

Now, make a list of the traits and gifts you bring into the Room.

If you want to be a little daring . . .

Write about—or speak aloud, alone with yourself—how you feel about all that you bring to God. What emotions do you experience when you think about bringing you, your personality traits, and your gifts into the Room with God?

How have others responded to you and the gifts you offer? And how have those responses affected how you feel now, entering this Room with God?

Find a comfortable place to lie down. Take several deep breaths to help relax your body. Now, imagine that you are looking down upon your physical self. What do you see? What is your emotional reaction to what you see?

Imagine that you are divine love looking down upon this physical self. Try to stay with this idea/image for several moments. Still your own thoughts and try to allow other thoughts to enter your mind—these are thoughts of God toward you as a physical person, as a woman of a specific age and race. What does God think of you?

The meeting place . . .

You come into the Room, where you will meet with God, and you know that there really is no need for a meeting place, because God has always been with you. God has always been in your coming and your going. You and I are alive, human beings in the world, only because God's Spirit gives us life. Even though we know all of that, we need the sense of relationship. And because we long for friendship, we seek a specific sort of place, a set-aside time, to intentionally nourish the awareness that for us is too often muted and invisible. This is why we come.

You are in the Room because it matters to you that God is present. It is rather unbelievable that God of the universe would permit any sort of knowing between you, but you are convinced—through sacred story, through the movement of Spirit, and through your own desire—that God wants your friendship. God desires you—the you who *is,* the you who contains all the pain and possibility of womanhood, the you who has failed as much as you've succeeded. The you who is, so many days, at war with herself.

Do you trust divine love to receive this complicated package you have become?

CHAPTER 8

Why is it hard to come to God?

While I kept silence, my body wasted away
through my groaning all day long.
For day and night your hand was heavy
upon me;
my strength was dried up as by the heat
of summer.

Psalm 32:3–4

We've talked already about how we try to manage life on our own, and about the containers we use when life spills over. Maybe you have decided *No, I cannot handle life on my own—I need God's help.* But you are not able to make the transition from holding on to letting go. Something gets in the way of your allowing God to handle what you cannot handle.

Let's imagine a twenty-something named Alicia, who has moved away from home and begun her own life. Her parents send her off with their blessings, knowing it's time for her to make her place in the world. They've told her many times that she can always come home if she needs help. She can pick up the phone and call and will always receive love and support.

As the months go by, however, Alicia communicates less and less, and her parents worry about this but don't press too much when she does infrequently call home. Nearly a year has gone by when they learn through an acquaintance that Alicia has recently moved from her apartment because she lost her job. She's living with a coworker in that faraway city while she looks for employment. Not only that, but she's lost weight and seems depressed—enough so that a friend of a friend has reported this back to Alicia's parents.

They are devastated to think that their daughter has gone through such difficulty without even mentioning it to them. They travel to that city to see their daughter, and only after they persist does she reveal that she had gotten involved with a man at her workplace, someone who mistreated her. She finally left the relationship, which meant leaving her job as well. She had become depressed and physically ill from the prolonged stress and heartbreak.

When her parents ask, "Why didn't you tell us?" what do you think she says? We can take our pick from several possibilities.

She's been in too much pain to discuss her situation with anyone. Emotionally she is so fragile that she must stay away from the topic simply to function while she looks for employment.

She's ashamed to have gotten into such a mess in the first place. Beyond the matter of getting intimately involved with someone outside of a committed relationship is the fact that she chose so unwisely a man whose treatment of her grew worse over time. She still can't bring herself to repeat some of the things he said to her or to recount the several instances when he hurt her physically.

She's too angry with her parents to trust them with any part of her life. This anger could be based on some disagreement or it could be a build-up of unspoken disappointments she's nursed secretly for years. Whatever the case, she expects her parents to respond to her with the same vindictiveness and distrust that she feels toward them.

She is afraid of changes she might have to make if she gets honest about her life. Maybe she really wants to make it on her own and so is unwilling to accept financial help even though she's become pretty desperate. Maybe she knows that her mother will urge her to see a counselor about this bad experience, especially if it involved physical abuse—and Alicia does not want to deal with counseling. Maybe a related problem is that she's managed her money badly all along, and she knows Dad will want to sit down with her and help come up with a plan.

In this hypothetical story, I've made it clear that Alicia's parents are supportive and loving, that they have done nothing to get in the way of relationship with their daughter. I have idealized them because, for our purposes, they represent God in relationship to us. It's never God who gets in the way of our growing relationship. It's always something on our end of the situation. Often our own emotional habits get in the way. Our psychological mindset can get in the way. Our memories and perceptions of spirituality can get in the way. And sometimes it's simply harsh life experience that makes it difficult for us to enter the Room and be open to God.

Alicia's dilemma provides four possible reasons people avoid help, whether the help of other people or the help of divine love.

We are overwhelmed by pain and don't know how to bring that pain to God. We might even think that the pain is somehow our own fault. We think that we must heal ourselves in order to come to God as the sort of person we want to be or that God expects us to be. Or we simply can't imagine that anything in heaven or earth could fix or heal the situation.

We are ashamed at our own failure and/or helplessness. We really thought we were better at dealing with life. We thought we'd progressed a little further as human beings. We are shocked at how easily we got off track or made a mess of things. We're humiliated by how we've allowed circumstances to get in the way of our progress.

We are profoundly disappointed or angry. Life so far has not turned out as we have expected or hoped, and the anger this causes is deep and powerful. We feel, at gut level, that God is responsible for our disappointment—God should have done something, should have protected us or stood up for us. One friend mentioned that she hesitates to come to God because too often she has "phoned home" only to get the answering machine. Sometimes God offers only silence and we are left with our questions, and our pain does not go away. We avoid God because we don't want to give the Divine any more opportunities to disappoint us. So, although at one level we long for friendship with God, we hold back.

We are afraid of what might happen if we truly open our souls to holiness and truth. Perhaps we have harbored shame for years and don't want to expose ourselves to more by discovering how far short we've fallen. Perhaps, after a lifetime of other people rejecting us, we fear that God will reject us, too. And sometimes we sense that in order to be friends with God we will have to change, and we don't want to.

Pain, shame, anger, and fear—are any of these operating in you? Do they slow down your steps as you approach the Room? Have they formed their own agendas in your soul, to the point that you don't really know what your deepest desires are?

There is no simple way to set aside such deeply abiding soul responses. Pain, shame, anger, and fear are real responses to real experience. They can lead us to act destructively, but to experience these responses does not make us bad or sinful people. If you are extremely afraid, that doesn't mean you must confess the fear as if you have, by your own choice, taken it as your stance toward life. Most of the time, these deep responses happen early in life and below our awareness, which is why we cannot handle them on our own. Which is why all we can do with pain, shame, anger, or fear is bring it with us into the Room. Deep soul responses require spiritual healing, and this sort of work is far beyond our abilities. This is the work that divine love accomplishes in us when we dare enter the Room and stay long enough for the work to happen.

*I used to avoid my dad when
I'd driven a splinter into finger or toe;
I knew he'd sterilize a needle and not stop
digging until the thing was out.
There must always be a cut or puncture,
I suppose because foul things never leave
on their own. Lord, I wouldn't mind
admitting what's in here if we could
deal with it minus the procedure.*

Here in the Room

If you are able, go for a walk. Get some fresh air and swing your arms and ask God's help as you assess your experiences with pain, shame, anger, and fear. Although you are walking around, really you are in the Room, that safe place for being honest. Divine love will assist you as you think about the deep soul responses that get in the way of your friendship with God. Divine love will remind you that you come to the Room not because you are healthy and whole but because you need to become healthy and whole.

If it would be helpful, finish the sentences that apply to you.

» God, I would be friends with you if only . . .
» God, you should know starting out that I am deeply, almost violently angry about . . .

» God, what I fear most about this whole friendship encounter is . . .

» God, I hurt so much, this feels impossible. I will try to describe what kind of pain I'm talking about.

We don't make these statements to help God understand us; God already understands our situations completely. We speak or write these things so that we can face them honestly and bring them to God intentionally.

I'll never forget the therapy session in which I finally admitted—at age thirty-something—that I was afraid of the dark. I spent a while describing all the scary things (real and imagined) of my childhood, and then went home feeling odd. Over the next days and weeks I discovered that I wasn't so scared after all. Merely speaking about those specific fears had done something inside me that felt almost miraculous. It really does make a difference when we speak the truth—to God or sometimes to another human being—about what is inside us.

CHAPTER 9

What happens if you fall apart?

Save me, O God,
  for the waters have come up to my neck.
I sink in deep mire,
  where there is no foothold;
I have come into deep waters,
  and the flood sweeps over me.
I am weary with my crying;
  my throat is parched.
My eyes grow dim
  with waiting for my God.

Psalm 69:1–3

Years ago, when my husband was struggling with debilitating depression, I attended for a while his sessions with a therapist, coming only to be present as silent support. One day the therapist said, "I know you don't have the capacity for hope right now. So I am going to carry that hope for you, until you're ready to carry it for yourself." What a gift that was, for another person to hold onto hope for us. It was as if hope was an extra heavy box that we could not handle on our own, and this kind man was going to carry it for as long as we needed him to do so.

This is a powerful image—someone else carrying what we cannot. It is just the image we need when life is too much for us. I can tell you one thing for sure: my life is too much for me.

I'll rephrase that: I cannot handle everything that comes my way. There was a time when I thought I could, if I just tried harder or prayed more or somehow figured out ahead of time how to be better prepared. When Jim's depression was at its worst, I still thought that our survival was mostly up to me. Of course God could help us—but I needed to be praying and supporting my husband and figuring out how to manage every aspect of our lives. I needed to be that wonderful person God could work through to help my husband.

Well, I had to get over that notion. It took several people to help put us back together again. Nowadays I'm much better at recognizing when I've come to the end of my own resources. I can say with little hesitation and no shame at all: my life is too much for me.

Forgive me if this sounds presumptuous, but I think your life is too much for you, too. Not because you're not good enough or strong enough or smart enough. Life is too much because we were never meant to hold within our individual souls all the amazement and terror and information and mystery that move through this universe every moment of our lives. The hosts of heaven are not the least bit surprised when we stumble around and fall apart.

If we are going to make friends with God, we need to get over the assumption that we can—or should—be successful and healthy to begin with. We need to release the idea that we must come to God fully formed or at least in good condition, spiritually or otherwise. When it comes to the growth of our souls, mainly what we do is allow God to work within us.

Actually, one of the first things that happens when we make connection with divine love is that we fall apart. Everything we have relied on—our intelligence and willpower and good intentions—fails as we try to lay hold of mystery. And only after we fail and fall apart are we in the position to deepen our friendship with God.

It is no small thing to be in the presence of the Holy. We may recall those Old Testament stories in which the people who were unlucky enough to physically touch the Ark of the Covenant (considered to be a form of God's presence among the people) were killed outright by the devastating power attached to the Ark. Moses went up the mountain to talk with God and came back down looking as if he'd been zapped with radiation. Back then, *nobody* wanted to be anywhere near God, let alone go into the Room to meet God. They knew that it was too much to take, that they would not survive the slightest touch from the Divine.

And still, many centuries removed from the stories of stone tablets and parting seas, we can survive contact with the Holy only because the Holy is ultimately merciful. God extends to us gentleness and speaks in words we can understand. When we come to God, we have no idea what we're doing, really. When we face God, it's all we can do to stay conscious, let alone hold on to our ideas and personal agendas.

God knows we will fall apart when confronted with the real presence of holiness and truth. That is why God has never expected us to handle what ordinary life gives us. God has always intended to provide for us what we need to survive reality. It's not enough, though, for God to provide for us; we have to allow God to handle for us what we cannot handle ourselves.

Over the years I've grown stronger and smarter in some ways, able to manage situations that I bungled before. But still the situation arrives that I'm no match for. Still my life is too much for me, but I don't have to do anything about that. All I need to do is come into the Room. And with me I bring hope, because some days hope is just too heavy and unwieldy, and so God will need to carry my hope, just as a wise therapist once did. I also bring pain, for although I've had a pretty good life, there is always a measure of pain in it. I understand now that often we cannot relieve our own pain. In fact, the worst pain must have help from outside. I bring to this Room my pain, and I set it down like a big rock and try not to keep picking it up or taking it back. My attitude now is "God, this is too much. This hurt is beyond my ability to bear or to heal."

It's important to remember, when we fall apart, that we are designed to be part of a community. Sometimes we must enter the Room with a good friend or counselor. Sometimes we need people praying for us while we're in the Room. Sometimes another human being is God's way of holding our hope when we can't.

So the question of the day is, how do you respond when you cannot handle your life? When you are falling apart, what is your first response? When you need hope you do not have, where do you find it?

One day it occurred to me that I had been
confessing the wrong sin. My sorrow
over chronic anxiety was misplaced
because, you see, I had many reasons
to be anxious. Life was, in fact,
so knotted and impossible that
I was amazed, in that moment
of clarity, that I wasn't more of a mess.
Ever since then I've come to God
on many a day with an odd smile
and the simple question:
"So, how will you fix this?"

Here in the Room

What do you do when you're unable to solve a problem?

What do you do when the stresses and emotions of the day make you incapable of thinking coherently?

Try now to write a little story—or tell the story with a series of pictures you draw or cut out of magazines. This is a story about you falling apart. It could be a true story, or one you make up. In fact, you might just try to imagine the worst that could happen in a situation. Imagine yourself without the usual supports or safety net. Try to work quickly and not analyze too much as you do this.

Now reflect on what it was like to imagine this kind of story. Then meditate for a few moments on this Scripture:

> Humble yourselves therefore under the mighty hand of
> God, so that he may exalt you in due time. Cast all your
> anxiety on him, because he cares for you.
>
> —*1 Peter 5:6–7*

What is your response to these words?

CHAPTER 10

What would it take to say yes to love?

Hear, O my people, while I admonish you;
    O Israel, if you would but listen to me! . . .
I am the LORD your God,
    who brought you up out of the land of Egypt.
    Open your mouth wide and I will fill it.

Psalm 81:8, 10

In the days when Jim and I were first dating, I became uncomfortable when he looked, or tried to look, into my eyes—you know, the way people do in the movies, gazing into the depths of each other's souls. For a long time I had wanted that sort of romantic scene in my life. And finally, here was this really nice guy trying to gaze across the table into my eyes, and I couldn't take it. I'd look away or, worse, giggle like a girl trying to be coy. I didn't want to be coy; I wanted this relationship to grow. But allowing this man to see me so directly was a new kind of

openness. It was unnerving to sense the energy that such connection created. I'm not talking so much about sexual energy; I
wasn't afraid of sex. It was the possibility of being truly known
that threw me into a panic.

After years of longing for love, we might just find that when
it shows up, we're not the least bit ready for it. We're not ready to
think of ourselves as beautiful and capable of loving well. We're
not ready to open ourselves to all the possibilities of that relationship—all the ways we might need to grow and get honest
and maybe get hurt. Saying yes to love is exhilarating, but it
can be terrifying, too. When we say yes, we relinquish any control we thought we had. Yes introduces possibility. In yes there
really is no limit, no wall to hit, no protective fences. Of course
true love protects the object of its love, but the relationship itself
enters a realm in which the potential for growth and exploration
is endless.

Saying yes to divine love will always lead to something. It
may compel us to change the way we look at life. Perhaps we've
become very skilled at self-loathing. Saying yes to God's love
means that we'll have to learn how to stop doing that. Saying yes
to love means that, sooner or later, we will love whomever God
loves—whether a member of our immediate family, a belligerent
next-door neighbor, or some orphan or widow or prisoner. God's
love is a transforming energy.

So we say yes to God's love. A door, reaching from here to
heaven, swings open.

We are so accustomed to conditional love. Some of us experienced this kind of love from one or both parents. Some of
us have suffered under the conditions placed on our marriage

by our spouse, or we have crippled the marriage with our own conditional love. For most of us, love has limits, love runs out of steam, love trips and falls, love even turns ugly. Our human experience rarely prepares us for the love God is waiting to lavish upon us.

> *Love is patient; love is kind; love is not envious or boastful or arrogant or rude. It does not insist on its own way; it is not irritable or resentful; it does not rejoice in wrongdoing, but rejoices in the truth. It bears all things, believes all things, hopes all things, endures all things. Love never ends.*
>
> —1 Corinthians 13:4–8

Saying yes to love means that we become more willing to take on impossible tasks in the name of love—tasks of healing and repairing, tasks of building and encouraging. It means that, in trying to do the impossible, we'll fail more than we used to because we're attempting to do more than we used to. God's love suffers failure and discomfort for the sheer sake of loving. God's love is not sidetracked by seasons of frustration and sorrow because love is worth every cost.

Saying yes to love means that we become more willing to be truly known, even though we suspect that some of what goes on inside us is not pretty. I often say that I thought I was a decent person—until I got married. Then it became clear who I'd really been all along: selfish and grasping, fearful, vindictive, judgmental, irritable. Allowing another person to know me deeply has been a consistently humbling experience. Likewise, in being

known by God we are saying yes not only to love but also to
humility.

All right, if I relent, if I say yes,
matters might just improve,
and I might even experience happiness,
which would be awkward for someone not
used to expecting much.
And also, if I say yes,
the day might disintegrate anyway
and drive home the truth that love
at its best will not always
make me happy,
which would be awkward for someone
so accustomed to measuring everything
by how easy it feels.

Here in the Room

Describe a time when love compelled you to go out on a limb, to try to do what seemed hopeless or impossible.

When you read the passage from 1 Corinthians 13 cited in this chapter, what reaction did it evoke in you?

Copy down the following Scripture on an index card or other small paper you can carry:

> I have loved you with an everlasting love;
>> therefore I have continued my faithfulness to you.
>>> —*Jeremiah 31:3*

For the next week, take this Scripture with you everywhere and read it several times a day.

PART THREE

Awareness

Perhaps it isn't surprising that when I began to really notice my breath, I began to really notice God. . . . I began to notice something else seemed to be there, not in the air or in the ground, but everywhere—something quiet and not at all pushy, some presence that seemed to be a part of me and yet not just me. Through breathing, I began to become aware that something was with me. . . . Sometimes it came on gently, and sometimes with a bodily and mental jerk. It was not threatening, but it was not human. It wasn't déjà vu, and it wasn't an overactive imagination. It was just there, an often overpowering sense of hugeness, a vastness that was, somehow, oddly familiar. It was gentle, but there was also no mistaking that it was massively powerful. It seemed, well, friendly. And when I was aware of it, I could not remember how I had not noticed it before.

KERRY EGAN, *FUMBLING*[3]

Jesus took the prophetic writings of Judaism beyond what people really expected. The Jews had dreamed of God's kingdom and the messiah who would usher it in. One day Jesus appeared and said simply, "The kingdom's already here." Suddenly, here was a prophet speaking in the present tense. Fulfillment wasn't off in the future but available right now.

This reality—that "the kingdom" is already here—is what makes it possible for us to be in relationship with God of the universe. The Divine has already broken into our existence and taken up residence with us. The grace and love of God infuse our breathing, walking, thinking, and dreaming. Jesus knew this. He recognized God's presence and activity when other people didn't perceive it at all.

Part of what Jesus came to do was show us what life could be like when we become aware of God among us. And because the Holy Spirit has come to dwell in us, we have received the permanent ability to perceive, in our everyday life, God's presence and movement.

CHAPTER 11

What is your history with God?

I will call to mind the deeds of the LORD;
   I will remember your wonders of old.
I will meditate on all your work,
   and muse on your mighty deeds.
Your way, O God, is holy.

Psalm 77:11–13

Spiritual and emotional healing can happen when we see Jesus with us in our pain. I've heard more than one story about someone with a history of deep trauma going back to a terrible memory—while in prayer or therapy—and seeing for the first time that she was not alone during the horror. Someone was with her, witnessing her suffering and grieving for her. We have a history with God whether or not we recognize it—and whether or not we consider ourselves friends of God.

The disciples who lived and traveled with Jesus did not clearly understand their relationship. They saw him as "master," a term any disciple would use for the rabbi who was training him, yet Jesus pointed out that he considered them his friends. They had a history with him, long days and nights of shared work and conversation, and still they tended to think of him as quite beyond them in his spiritual giftedness. Perhaps he was even the Messiah. They could not readily see the relationship for what it was—true friendship.

We usually operate under the misconception that because we don't feel close to God, then God is not close to us. We think that because we have not been more intentional about our relationship with the Divine, then that relationship is inactive, or even dead. Actually, God has always been active in our life, has treated us lovingly time and again. But have we been aware of that?

We don't always see divine love for what it is, because we have little room in our personal systems for love that is undeserved, that isn't in some way the reward for good living or sharpened consciousness. We may assume that, in order for God to love us, we must become better people, more deserving of that love. If we think this way—and often this sort of attitude is more subconscious than conscious—then we can miss God's daily acts of love.

By its very nature, friendship is reciprocal; one friend loves the other, and the other recognizes that love, acknowledges it, and returns it. We can't participate in a true friendship with

God until we recognize God's love toward us. Once that begins to happen, we are able to respond to that love. The miracle is that a human being can be in a reciprocal relationship with the Divine at all. By reciprocal I don't mean equal; God loves us in ways we could never match. But our Creator has deemed it good and possible for us to respond to divine love and for relationship to develop.

If you seek now to be in friendship with the Divine, you can choose to acknowledge God's presence already with you, and to respond to that presence. You can do this in a number of ways; one is to look back at your history with fresh perspective.

What a surprise—to see you
in the story I wrote at age fourteen,
or in the turmoil I entered willingly
in order to help a friend, or a stranger.
How delightful—to remember a song
or a word that described, exactly,
how wonderful was your love.
And all the time I considered these
mere daydreams, little wishes of mine.

Here in the Room 🍵
A map of significant moments . . .

Now you're going to focus on the significant moments of your life. For our purposes, a significant moment is any time/event when you sensed the strong pull of divine love. These were moments in which

>> you experienced a sharp, unmistakable desire to connect with God or with authentic spirituality as you understood it

>> you became acutely aware of God's presence, through an overwhelming sense of peace, gratitude, love, awe, or joy

>> you understood clearly and powerfully something about your spiritual life

>> you discovered an answer you had been looking and/or praying for

>> you witnessed divine love and power in a situation, such as rescue from danger or the healing of illness

>> you experienced vivid awareness of life's wonder/mystery/ beauty

>> you were able to accomplish something far beyond your own means

>> you were able to bear something far beyond your own strength or endurance

>> you witnessed a change of circumstance that seemed miraculous

>> you were touched to the core by a work of art, which turned simple appreciation into an occasion for transcendence

» your spirit was awakened mightily by a song, a passage of Scripture, or the words of someone speaking

» you knew, suddenly and unmistakably, what you needed to do, what the next step of your journey would be

» you received the help you needed, possibly before you even knew you needed it

» another person, for no particular reason, committed an outlandish act of love or kindness, for you

Perhaps you would not have named God specifically in connection with these moments or events, but it is safe to say that you were touched in a memorable way by something benevolent that lay beyond you and your abilities. Even when other people come to our aid or say something powerful enough to help us, we have in fact been helped by God's love hovering over the world, the same love that created the world and that still tends and nourishes it today.

If you want to go a bit deeper . . .

Imagine that each of these significant moments has been captured on film—as a scene from a movie or photographs in an album. Spend some time with the memory of each moment, and describe on paper—whether through words, illustrations, or pictures you've cut out of magazines—each scene or photograph. You might want to use one piece of paper for each moment, so that you can put them in chronological order, arranged as a timeline on the floor or table or pinned up on the wall. Or you might make them small pages and turn them into a little photo album or memory book.

If you feel a little daring . . .

Invite a spiritual helper to dwell with you for a while and talk with you about each of these scenes or pictures, these significant moments from your life. This spiritual helper can be God (the Father, Mother, Creator . . .), the Holy Spirit, Jesus, Mary, a saint or angel, or a loved one who is deceased. Do your best to sit still and simply listen to your spiritual helper. It takes discipline not to break in and offer your own ideas; stay quiet now so that you can receive insight and revelation from beyond yourself.

Or, discuss your significant moments with a close friend or a spiritual director, taking care to listen more than you speak.

CHAPTER 12

How can Jesus help your God-awareness?

He chose his servant David,
   and took him from the sheepfolds;
from tending the nursing ewes he brought him
   to be the shepherd of his people Jacob. . . .
With upright heart he tended them,
   and guided them with skillful hand.

Psalm 78:70–72

When I was in junior high, a new girl joined my class—I'll call her Jan—and we struck up a friendship. As time went on, I tried to introduce her to Christianity. She was interested in spirituality but didn't want to hear about God the Father. My main perception of God was as heavenly Father, possibly because my own dad was so prominent in my life. After Jan and I had been friends for some time, she revealed that her father had committed suicide the year before she moved to our town. She didn't say so then, but I came to understand that for Jan, "father" meant abandonment and unnameable pain. During high school, Jan came to faith by befriending Jesus; eventually she was able to get acquainted with God as parent too.

For many people, Jesus is the one who awakens their awareness to divine love. And if we are going to make friends with God, we can't escape encountering Jesus, who tempers and perfects everything we know about God. By his life, death, and resurrection, Jesus changed forever the human experience of God. Thanks to Jesus, we have a better understanding of who God is.

When we try to resist the Divine by considering God distant and uninvolved with us, there is Jesus, taking time with individual people, physically touching them, meeting their gaze, listening intently, finding just the right words to say. If Jesus is God-in-the-flesh, then how he attended to people was a brilliant revelation of how God attends to us.

When we get caught up in tedious debates, hammering away at issues until faith has become practically one-dimensional, there is Jesus with his encouragement to stop worrying about what is unimportant anyway, or his forthright admonishment to forgive people if we ever hope to move forward spiritually.

When we distort God into a rigid moralist, a cosmic policeman, or a nagging parent, Jesus reminds us that a loving father won't give his children a stone when they ask for bread. No matter what crazy direction we try to run with our ideas about God, Jesus is ahead of us, sitting there in the sunshine cooking us breakfast.

When we encounter Jesus as God's very presence in human form, we may be able to approach God in friendship more easily.

Because Jesus walked, talked, ate, slept, and maneuvered through life just as we must, we can imagine God as an entity we might actually relate to.

But there's another aspect of Jesus that can truly set us free for friendship with God. It's easy to think of Jesus as divine, God-in-person. A fully divine Jesus should have no problem becoming friends with God; of course he could pray and work miracles. But Jesus was fully human, too. *And as a human being, Jesus had to learn—just as you and I do—how to live as a friend of God.*

The Gospel writers point out that Jesus regularly went off by himself to spend time in prayer. In the midst of demanding work, he gave up sleep to go out early in the morning to be in the Room with his heavenly Father. This is *Jesus Christ* we're talking about, needing to go into the Room! By some miracle and mystery, Jesus the Divine was able to encounter God as Jesus the human being who had to learn day by day how to participate more fully in relationship with the Divine.

Jesus did not come to earth fully formed, knowing everything that was going to happen to him and having all wisdom and power automatically, as though he were little more than a human robot God used to carry out a plan. Because Jesus was born a baby, grew up through the normal stages of human development, and lived one day at a time as we do, he learned bit by bit what it meant to be in friendship with God. He grew into his faith as his family taught him the great traditions of Judaism. He grew into awareness of his work in the world as he spent regular time putting himself in the Room with God, whom he called "Dad."

So, when it comes to friendship with God, Jesus serves us in two ways. He gives us an incarnation of divine life that we can relate to—we can make friends with God by making friends with Jesus, which to many of us is more plausible than befriending God the Father or Creator. And we can also follow Jesus' example in becoming friends with God. We can watch Jesus the human relate to God the divine parent, and we can do as he did.

In the beginning I imagined you
handsome and quiet, wandering
the world one good deed to the next,
a savior ever calm, with ample wisdom
for my problems. You were my Jesus,
who understood me, stood up for me,
helped me.
Along the way something changed.
To see you weep in the darkness,
struggle up a hill, and choke to death
threatened my confidence for a few years.
Now it's the struggle, the painful growth,
even the failure of death
that draws me to you.
This is a life I recognize,
one I can trust. In fact, I sense you
close by these days, through every hour
in which I feel lost or desperately thirsty
or barely able to take a step.

Here in the Room ☕_____

Read this story from the Gospel of Luke, and reread portions as you ponder the questions below.

> As [Jesus] went, the crowds pressed in on him. Now there was a woman who had been suffering from hemorrhages for twelve years; and though she had spent all she had on physicians, no one could cure her. She came up behind him and touched the fringe of his clothes, and immediately her hemorrhage stopped. Then Jesus asked, "Who touched me?" When all denied it, Peter said, "Master, the crowds surround you and press in on you." But Jesus said, "Someone touched me; for I noticed that power had gone out from me." When the woman saw that she could not remain hidden, she came trembling; and falling down before him, she declared in the presence of all the people why she had touched him, and how she had been immediately healed. He said to her, "Daughter, your faith has made you well; go in peace."
>
> —*Luke 8:42–48*

Consider Jesus the human being . . .

At what point is it clear that Jesus' perception of the situation is different from that of the people around him?

The fact that Jesus has sensed power, or energy, leave him, suggests that he must be acutely aware of his physical life. Think of your own body, and the way it sometimes speaks to you. What helps your physical awareness? What practices can you imagine Jesus using from day to day in order to dwell so completely in his own body that he can be physically sensitive to the people who come to him?

Consider Jesus the divine person . . .

A woman with a hemorrhage was considered unclean in that time and culture; her illness has cut her off from social participation for more than a decade. She's probably endangering herself by confessing to everyone there why she touched Jesus. I imagine that she trembles partly because she has felt a healing occur but also because she fears the crowd and maybe even Jesus.

Imagine that you have suffered from reproductive disorders for twelve years. You can't have babies, you're constantly losing blood, and you've had it up to here with the medical industry. You manage to make tangible contact with Jesus, and he looks into your eyes and says, "Daughter, your faith has made you well. Go in peace."

What do Jesus' words and actions reveal about God's response to you?

CHAPTER 13

How do you live in the space you're given?

How lovely is your dwelling place,
O Lord of hosts! . . .
For a day in your courts is better
than a thousand elsewhere.
I would rather be a doorkeeper in the
house of my God
than live in the tents of wickedness.

Psalm 84:1, 10

After years of working full-time in the publishing industry, I had the opportunity to cut back to part-time work in order to do more of my own writing. In addition, I had permission from my employer to do about half of my work from home, eliminating from my schedule hours of commuting. In anticipation of a super-productive life, I carefully divided the space on the huge desk (actually, sheets of plywood across cinder blocks) that covered one end of our dining room: editing work in one section, household business in another, freelance projects in another, and my creative stuff in yet another.

Within a month, I was so depressed I could barely move. Jim scheduled an appointment with our therapist, and I went reluctantly, knowing that nothing on earth could lift the darkness. I told the therapist about this wonderful situation I had, being able to write more—and yet I was failing completely, at writing and everything else. By the end of the session we had a simple plan. I would go back to the office to edit, and I would find a different space in which to do freelance work. My writing needed a space of its own. The solution seemed too simple to be effective, but within weeks everything was better. And I had learned an important lesson about the dynamics of space and place.

Each of us works and lives within physical confines. We may like our current space, or we may be trying to upgrade our situation. If we live in a recently built suburban housing development, we probably have the kind of space our grandparents would have shared with grown children and grandchildren; if we live in the heart of a large city, we'll do well to have a one-bedroom apartment with enough room to turn around in. The question is: How do we dwell in that space? What kind of awareness do we bring to the physical places of our life?

This matter is particularly relevant to women, because we continue to be the primary forces that make and shape "home." We instinctively value what home feels like, looks like, smells like, tastes like, and sounds like. Because so many of us have children and tend to their growing up, we place a lot of importance upon the physical spaces our families live in. We understand at an intuitive level that physical location makes a real difference in how people experience day-to-day living.

In the Old Testament, God gave specific instructions to Moses about how to construct the tabernacle, where God would dwell with the people of Israel. And the temple built by Solomon was famous for its majesty and beauty and the richness of its materials. These structures were important, not only because of their religious significance, but because people need places that are intended just for them and for specific purposes. The people needed a room in which to smell incense, admire the colorful tapestries, hear the prayers, and so forth. From earliest times, people understood that God could not be contained by a physical dwelling, but that wasn't the point. We are given this amazing ability to create spaces in such a way that *we* are better able to attend to God's beauty and to the details of life.

I have learned to work with space more intentionally than I used to, designating certain spaces in my home for certain activities. This helps me focus on the activity at hand rather than worry about other activities I'm not doing at the moment. So there's a room where I do only my creative work. It's a tiny room, but that's all I need. In the apartment we used to have, my creative place was the corner of our bedroom, where I kept a comfortable chair and all my writing stuff. I didn't edit or pay bills in that chair, just as I don't edit or pay bills in my writing room now.

Usually the "office" area of the house is piled high and looks desperate, but that means that other areas of the house are free of business/bill clutter. Space will always bring limits with it, but

I try to truly dwell in the space I'm given and to make it work for the priorities I've chosen. So, rather than becoming distracted by the rambling country house I would have if I were rich—or reconfiguring my and my husband's work life so that we could afford a luxurious home but never be home to enjoy it—I use the various spaces in our little house to help focus my energy and attention. This is something I began to learn years ago when our living space was much smaller, and I try to hold on to those lessons now in the present home as I face my endless capacity to want more.

More often than we realize, we lose precious energy through a fairly constant, if not quite conscious, dissatisfaction with the space we're given. We fight space because of its limitations when we could use space as the gift it is.

Another problem with fighting our limits is that we can use our situation to excuse the neglected state of our souls. We might think, *If I had a better place to pray, I'd do it more.* Or, *If only I could live up in the mountains, or somewhere close to the ocean, I know I could connect better with God.* This sort of thinking just gets in the way of all the wonder we could experience. God is not waiting for a more scenic spot in which to meet you. God knows that, no matter where you live, the Room is inside you anyway.

When we try to approach the Divine with spiritual companionship in mind, we need our best attention. We must practice mental and emotional focus. Most of all, we have to learn to be at home right where we are; otherwise we will fidget away our time and never quite connect with this very crucial process of being with God.

So wherever we are is—at least today—the place that really matters. How do we regard that place? What will we do with it, and how will we use it to sharpen our awareness of divine presence in our days and nights?

For instance, maybe there's a chair that's really comfortable, where we enjoy reading or just being. Maybe it's the spot where we tuck away a journal, or where we knit or sketch to help us relax and think and plan.

There is a chair by the window
in a small room near the back of my house,
where sitting is a form of art-making.
In that place I do very well at doing
nothing at all. I can address the midday
light as one greets angels coming and going.
From the smooth bowls of half-melted candles
I can scoop out the scent of wise thoughts.
Prayers form in the sleepy corners of my eyes.
In that chair I must stop, and keep stopping,
because there always seems to be something
about to happen, or on the verge
of being known. Did I mention how
the books and pets gather round?

Here in the Room 🍵

Try to draw a diagram of the spaces that contain most of your living: workplace, house, yard, or neighborhood park. This drawing can be rough and without much detail.

Circle or highlight the spaces that are most crucial to you and your various roles. My "hot" spots would be my desk at work, my writing room at home, our kitchen, and the areas where we are together most, such as bedroom, family room, or back porch.

For each of your hot spots, try to draw a more detailed diagram, as if you are hovering above that space and looking down at it. Draw a circle around each hot spot, setting it apart from the others.

Once you have these separate, more detailed diagrams to look at, you can use them in a number of ways. You might want to assess the way they're laid out. My husband and I have decided recently to work more with the elements of our tiny office, because we don't do much there but pile and file things; we might use the space better if we do some rearranging. Knowledge of feng shui could help!

What you are doing is approaching your various physical spaces with more intention and reflection. You are receiving them as yours for the time being (you never know when life will bring change to your spaces). You can do any of the following, or add possibilities as you like:

» Make a new blueprint for the layout of a space.

» Set a time to enter a specific space in order to clean and sort it out so that it will better reflect its purpose.

» Pray over a specific space, in a manner similar to the way people hold blessing services for a new home or building. This can be a solitary or group affair. For instance, if there's a baby on the way, how appropriate to spend time praying in the nursery or other areas in the house that will be important to the newborn. If you have decided to give more energy to your creative gifts, you might want to pray over your creative space and furnish it in a way that's most conducive to your creativity. Or, if someone is coming to stay with you for a while, pray over the hospitality to be expressed throughout the home.

» Spend time with the diagram of each space, writing key phrases, Scripture verses, poetry, or your thoughts about that space. You might color it with crayons, pencils, or markers. If you enjoy working with mandalas, you can treat each diagram as one—you've already drawn a circle around it. The point is to work with the space visually and conceptually.

» Go physically into each space and pay particular attention to objects, colors, and lighting.

As you work more intentionally with the physical spaces in your life, you will probably find that you are dwelling more comfortably and consciously in your life generally. As you dwell better in your life, you will do less fidgeting and fighting. This will enhance all your relationships, including your friendship with God.

A room for the Room . . .

Don't be surprised if you begin creating a space especially for your time in the Room. Many of us prefer to meet with God in specific places and even at specific times. This has nothing to do with God's "location" but has much to do with our own ability to focus and to attend to divine presence.

Don't be surprised if your physical room for God is not what you expected. At different times I have felt more connected and focused upon divine presence in the bathtub, in a living room chair, in my writing room, and—lately—on the commuter train. Eventually, with practice and attention, we will be able to perceive God's presence with us anywhere and at any time. We may believe that God is always present, but that doesn't mean we are able to attend to that presence; this awareness is partly gift and partly the fruit of our own practice. It pleases me these days that I sense God's presence so often when I'm in the midst of strangers on the way to work—how fitting for an introvert! How like the Holy Spirit to affect me most strongly in a crowd rather than where I am usually most comfortable.

When I work with writers and other artists, we often discuss our creative space—the physical locations we use for our work. I encourage people to do whatever they must to help them engage with the creative process. Some people light a candle, others keep certain objects around them, while others need music playing in the background. At the same time, I remind them that these are merely practices—habits we build that help us engage—and that a practice that works now may not work at another time in life.

So even as you work with the various spaces in your life, and as you construct a physical environment that assists you in your friendship with God, keep in mind that the holy relationship will always transcend physical reality. Depending on your personal history, habits, and character traits, working with physical space will be meaningful or not. For some people, physical space won't be an issue at all, whereas other individuals are quite sensitive to environment and must work with it in anything they do.

If you want to go a little deeper . . .

Create a blessing for every physical space that is meaningful to you. Invite a friend to perform the blessings along with you. Make an occasion out of it, ending with a meal or some other celebration. There is a lot to celebrate, after all. Divine love has gifted you with a place in which to dwell, and grow, and increase in love.

CHAPTER 14

How will you react to the realities of time?

A thousand years in your sight
   are like yesterday when it is past,
   or like a watch in the night.
You sweep them away; they are like a dream,
   like grass that is renewed in the morning;
in the morning it flourishes and is renewed;
   in the evening it fades and withers.

Psalm 90:4–6

Women have biological clocks: our bodies mark off the months and tick away the years of our fertility. Because so many of us care for small children, we measure a year or a decade by the length of their limbs, the extent of their vocabularies, and the growing complexity of their daily achievements. Because so many of us care for elderly family members, we mark our days by the morning, noon, afternoon, evening, and bedtime zones for medications and other routines. And for centuries our communities have kept track of their hours by the meals we prepared and set before them. Women understand time. We live in constant awareness of its passing.

You would think that, given our devoted attention to time, it would treat us more kindly. But we are mortal after all, and our physical systems soon start their slow but inexorable deterioration. For the woman who has not had children but wants to, the anxiety begins to build around age thirty. Will she find the right partner in time? Or, if she has already found that partner, will pregnancy endanger her newly flourishing career? Will she be fertile? And what will she do if she is not?

For the woman who wants a significant relationship she does not yet have, every passing year represents potential partners disappearing from her future. Meanwhile, should she buy a home, spend resources traveling and having fun without a partner, or change location—and community—yet again to accommodate a career that promises to bloom if tended properly?

Physical signs of aging frighten some of us. We have been taught that appearance is an important factor in love, and we believe that vitality is indispensable at work. Some of us sag sooner than others, but even those who retain more youthful looks feel the years in muscle and bone. When midlife arrives, our hormonal systems shift according to their own predetermined schedule. Some days a woman feels absolutely trapped inside her body, this entity that seems to go its own way with no regard for how she might feel about it.

The world often begins to come apart during the middle years. Our children are old enough now to truly complicate our lives by the decisions they make. Our parents become ill or die. We may face major surgery or adjustments in lifestyle. And because our significant others are usually experiencing a similar midlife angst, we are likely to face relational problems as well— major fractures or even divorce. We fear becoming plain, dumpy, ugly—or worse, invisible. We're not sure how we will carry on once our society ceases to recognize us as sexual or significant.

The later years bring with them still more challenges to health and peace of mind. We may have retired, but we still want to be fruitful. What good can we do now that we are out of the mainstream, living in a world shaped by much younger people? How active can, or should, we be in the lives of our children and grandchildren? For many of us, an additional challenge of the senior years is learning to live alone after our spouse has died. Now we must become acquainted with yet another version of ourselves, and do we have the energy or imagination for such an overhaul?

Time forces us to look at ourselves more honestly. We may begin to see that we are not nearly as strong as we had thought. As our youth and beauty fade, our supporting structures crumble. Here we thought we had faith and purpose, only to discover that mainly we are desperate to fix our bellies and upper arms. Is it any wonder, then, that time's passing catapults so many of us into a phase of high spiritual energy?

Whatever our age, we say to ourselves one day, looking in the mirror or struggling to survive yet another shift, "I'm running out of time." And the fear travels up our spine like a sudden chill. This sort of fear has the power to drive us to craziness: affairs, divorce, plastic surgery, new wardrobes, and expensive toys. Or we can use the energy of that fear to drive us inward, to the root of our reality. This is a great time to run into the Room where God's friendship dwells. Divine love has patiently waited for us to loosen our grip on our tangible if faulty supports.

Sometimes a girl has to go through multiple dazzling men before she finally settles down with the right man. And sometimes we ignore the friendship God offers because we just think other activities will be more interesting. Fortunately for us, God welcomes our love at any stage or time. Even if we have frittered away the most productive years of our lives on ambition and simple busyness, when we face our mortality at last and know that better financing will not save us, it is still possible to change direction.

In fact, over the years most of us have acquired the skill and self-awareness to pursue God with more focus than ever. Now we are harder to fool; we've been around the block a few times, and when we decide to pursue a more substantial relationship with God, we are better equipped to do so. We know ourselves better; we are more willing to admit, up front, where we have failed and are weak. We have developed better radar for stupidity and fraud. And, frankly, we don't have time to waste, which helps some of us become more decisive and discerning.

When we realize that we can no longer ignore the limits of time, some of us become almost fearless about faith. No matter what we were taught or conditioned to believe, we are willing to let go of it in the interest of finding the truth. We don't have time for propaganda and falsehood.

In the eyes of divine grace, we truly do get better with age. Even as our physical vitality diminishes and our outward beauty

fades, we are brimming with spiritual potential. When we dare
to grapple with the reality of time, many of us break through to
new planes of spirituality altogether. We finally learn how to
pray with quieter, more open hearts. We are able to take the time
to truly meditate. We don't feel the pressure to always have an
opinion or to always voice the opinions we have.

Time doesn't have to be the enemy; it can be a catalyst, urg-
ing us by its passing to let go of the trivial and concentrate on
what really matters. To be honest, I wasn't so concerned about
being God's friend a decade or two ago; I was too busy getting
things done, trying to be productive, fussing with my hair, and
worrying about what people thought of me. The passing of precious time is bringing about a gradual reversal. Time sifts us,
sorts our loves, and reorders our priorities. For this alone, we
have much reason to hope.

I never expected glory to appear
between the waiting and the wanting.
I did not look for redemption in
repeated failures; yet is my life saved
again and again.
And time circles round, a wild spinning
wind that grabs my shirt and
ruffles my plans.
In the always goingness of time
is a lightness, a loosening grip,
a slipping sensibility that feels,
against all reason, lovely.

Sometimes in the last moments of sleep
I sense a great lifting upon the wave
that never stops surging forward and
upward, flinging us out of time
into all our longings—those we have named
and those for which we have no words.

Here in the Room

Find some materials for drawing—paper and markers, pencils, or crayons. Get comfortable, perhaps with a favorite beverage to help you relax and concentrate, and enter the mindset of taking enough time to relax with this project.

Look at your life in seasons. They could be typical seasons: spring (childhood), summer (young adulthood), fall (middle age), winter (old age). Or they could be seasons you label arbitrarily. For instance, I could label the seasons of my timeline like this:

> » first spiritual formation (childhood through high school)
> » first career (years in music school and as a music teacher)
> » second spiritual formation (about a decade during which I left the faith of my first formation and discovered a new life of faith)
> » second career (editing and writing)

We might label the seasons according to relationships:
> » childhood friendships
> » high-school friendships

» first boyfriend
» college friendships
» single young adulthood
» marriage and friendships past young adulthood
» expanding family (children and their children, siblings and their families)
» mentoring years (senior at workplace, grandmother)
» single senior in assisted living

A person could label seasons according to the difficulties he or she has endured:

» childhood survival of serious family dysfunction
» marriage too early that was filled with strife and ended in divorce
» fighting cancer
» caring for aging, infirm parents
» dealing with son, who was in so much trouble
» loneliness after retirement

Or, in a more positive vein, we could label seasons according to gifts and accomplishments:

» volunteering in community theater and youth outreach
» having a family and nurturing children
» developing programs and writing articles
» working for a company and becoming more financially stable
» exploring deeper spiritual practices and trimming work schedule in order to do more volunteer work.

If you have the time and feel so inclined, sketch out your life in several different ways, changing the way you label seasons each time. The purpose is to step away from your personal experience and gain more objectivity about what you have done and when.

Circle of life . . .

In order to do this exercise, you'll need blank paper without lines and something round to trace, such as a pan lid or salad plate. Draw a circle that's at least six inches across, possibly eight or ten inches across. This is your mandala—the circle that represents the whole of your life in terms of time. Divide it into sections, like pieces of a pie, but they don't need to be equal in size. In fact they shouldn't be, because each section represents a significant season of your life. Inside each section you're going to draw a symbol that best communicates what that season was like for you.

Please remember that you're not dead yet. Only part of your circle will be sectioned off and labeled. You may expect to go through two or three more seasons yet, and you can draw symbols in them for what you expect those seasons to be like.

Now, draw some little faces in each section of your mandala. These are the faces of the significant people who have accompanied you during the respective life seasons. If you need to, name the faces.

If you want to be a little daring . . .

Mark your mandala to indicate God's presence during those seasons. This marking can be in the form of symbols. You also might shade each season a color that expresses for you how God's presence felt to you during that season. Or provide a song title—your selections could range from "How Great Thou Art" to "What Have You Done for Me Lately?"

CHAPTER 15

What are your harmful attachments?

They soon forgot [God's] works;
  they did not wait for his counsel.
But they had a wanton craving in the
    wilderness,
  and put God to the test in the desert;
he gave them what they asked,
  but sent a wasting disease among them.

Psalm 106:13–15

I once knew a woman of impeccable taste who spent most of her adult life serving Christian communities in Middle Eastern countries. I wondered how someone who loved pretty things so much could deal with all the moving around (Jordan, Lebanon, Cyprus) and with the guaranteed periodic loss of home and possessions, given how often items got lost or broken in transit. Her simple answer was that she enjoyed nice things, but they were just things, and if she lost them she could always go buy something else. She had learned the balance of enjoying her life in every detail without getting inordinately attached to furniture, mementos, or houses. To some extent she had to hold relationships lightly as well, while forming real friendships along the way, because her community, by its very nature, shifted every few years.

Ignatian spirituality uses the term *disordered attachment* to describe any emotional, mental, or spiritual attachment that gets in the way of spiritual growth. Here are a few of the more common ones:

Standard of living. Some of us must let go of our ideas about how much money is enough. If we don't, then our "need" for money can compel us to take jobs we shouldn't take, work longer hours than is beneficial for our families, and borrow money we don't have in order to obtain the stuff or finance the improvements we don't need.

Relationships. If we are too attached to our relationships (or to the futures they promise), we become clingy, jealous, defensive, and fearful. Who hasn't pushed for a romance to proceed further than it seemed to be going? Who hasn't panicked when a friend became distant and stopped coming around so much? What parent hasn't tried too hard to make a child do and say the things that made the parent feel less anxious and more loved?

Much-loved processes. This is a common issue in organizations, whether workplaces or parishes. We finally get the kinks out of a system when a new manager decides we need another one entirely. We know that the way our committee organizes church hospitality is so good it's practically ordained by God—why would anyone want to change it?

Outcome of a decision. So, will you get the job or not? Will the bank approve the loan or not? Will the powers-that-be pass the proposal so that you can get started on important work? Will your spouse agree to counseling or to finally getting a check-up? Will your child get accepted into the school of your choice?

Geographic location. Are you willing to leave your beloved neighborhood, friends, workplace, church, and so on—if your participation with God tugs you somewhere else? Are you willing to give up a perfectly good situation because a family member's health requires it? (Could I leave my bungalow and little garden, after I waited so long to have them?)

Well-loved activities. Yes, we should pay attention to what we truly enjoy doing, because those activities probably feed us in a good way. But appetites are greedy, and it's not unusual for a friend of God to find herself curtailing favorite pastimes in order to be more present to other people, spend more time in solitude or prayer, or otherwise be about God's business in the world. For instance, I love my solitude; I could spend hours alone in my writing room immersed in books and tapping away on the laptop. But I happen to be married, and no matter how satisfying it feels to be in my cave with my favorite things, I must unattach regularly, even if that means plopping down in the family room to watch *Law & Order* reruns with my husband. I prefer long train rides for reading but sometimes need to accept someone's offer of a ride because it's important to open my life to that person a little more, if only for a thirty-minute conversation.

I know I am too attached to something when I feel threatened by its potential loss. When I can sense myself beginning to claw my way to a desired outcome, it's time to sit in the Room and ask God's help. Desperation of any kind skews the way a person thinks and acts—and disordered attachments always have a whiff of desperation about them.

Disordered attachments are sometimes bad habits, such as addiction, self-hatred, or the compulsive need to control people and situations. A disordered attachment can be our need to always feel safe or to always have others' approval. When we live as God's friends, sometimes we end up in unsafe places because that's where God needs us to offer divine love and healing. When we live as God's friends, we will most certainly upset some of the people whose approval we used to enjoy, because God's work in the world is always founded on an honest assessment of things, and people don't always welcome the truth.

When we face our disordered attachments, we move toward a state called *detachment* by some, *indifference* by others. Don't let those words fool you: the solution to disordered attachment is not the refusal to care or be involved. When we manage our attachments, we become freer to truly love. We can let go and love others, or let go and love God—or let go and love ourselves.

I once bought a leather cap in a Turkish bazaar. I loved that cap so much that whenever I left the house but didn't wear it, I would hide it. If thieves broke in,

they might take the books and clothes
but would not find my cap!
I did not understand then that
I went to elaborate lengths to hide the cap
because I was lonely, I lived halfway across
the world, and could not speak the language.
Years later, I decided that the cap
no longer flattered me,
so I let it go to rummage.
On that same trip I bought a tapestry coat,
which I wore for a decade or more.
But one day, a woman on the commuter
train complimented its richness,
her eyes filling with light.
It wasn't hard at all to give her the coat.
I sent with it my long happiness
in having worn it.
So today, I have neither the cap nor the coat.
It's easy to say which one I think of
most often. It's not the cap.

Here in the Room

Fear is a great indicator of disordered attachment because it focuses upon what we don't want to lose or give up. Ask yourself now, When am I afraid? What situations trigger my fear?

What kinds of loss or change are most threatening to you? Can you spend time imagining potential situations that would threaten your attachments?

Please remember that attachments are often simply love out of balance. It's wonderful to enjoy a good meal with friends—but must you always go to an expensive restaurant or spend days cooking to provide the perfect feast? It's good that you are a loyal friend, but does that loyalty lead you to expect total devotion in return? Getting unattached means holding life lightly and with tempered expectations.

Think of all the things you love and try to determine where some of those loves may be out of balance.

Invite the Trinity to sit with you while you imagine your attachments falling away. There's Jesus, who had to learn detachment, too, when he lived a human life. There's God your parent-creator, who knows exactly how you are put together and who understands what is utterly best for the whole of your life. There's the Holy Spirit, who longs for your soul to be at peace and for you to enjoy complete freedom to live well. Listen to what God-in-three-persons has to say to you.

PART FOUR

Resistance

I have wasted the better part of my life in vanities, . . . in vain pleasures and in foolish illusions. . . . There are immense voids in my life: I have not always done my duty to my neighbor, or to the members of my family. . . . Instead of seeking God, I have sought myself. I have desired comforts, I have been vainglorious and obstinate in defending my own opinion. . . . What touchiness, cowardice and uncharitableness! O my Jesus, it makes me tremble when I consider that it is the end of the day, that night is coming on, and that my heart, alas! remains full of vices, stains and iniquities!

CONCEPCIÓN CABRERA DE ARMIDA,

BEFORE THE ALTAR[4]

If we are designed for friendship with God, then why is it such a struggle to develop that friendship? If God desires our company, and if we possess an inherent desire for God, won't things simply take their course?

Entire theologies delve into this topic, which falls under the general category of sin and repentance. But those words are loaded terms, weighted with much history and interpretation. It's simpler to speak in terms of resistance. We resist God. We avoid true contact with the Divine, and we do so for many reasons.

CHAPTER 16

What is holding you back?

> How often they rebelled against him
>   in the wilderness
>   and grieved him in the desert!
> They tested God again and again,
>   and provoked the Holy One of Israel.
> They did not keep in mind his power,
>   or the day when he redeemed them
>   from the foe.
>
> Psalm 78:40–42

People will always give reasons for their misbehavior. He had an affair because sex with his wife had grown dull or non-existent. She embezzled from her employer to avoid foreclosure on her house. He was abusive to a coworker because he was under stress. She neglected her children because she was exhausted.

The same goes for our behavior toward God. We don't pray because we can't deal with patriarchal images of the Divine. We ignore moral principles because of the hurtful people we associate with lists of dos and don'ts. We turn away from divine invitation to friendship because we are too hurt, angry, ashamed, or afraid.

There is a whole realm of resistance, however—I call it the Big Resistance—that works in us apart from fear, anger, pain, perception, or experience. This resistance is not forced upon us but seems to grow up within us like persistent weeds in an otherwise lovely garden. This is what theologians—and standard Christian doctrine—call sin. This resistance is our tendency to move away from God, even as our souls yearn to move closer to God.

The Jewish and Christian traditions offer the story of Adam and Eve in the Garden of Eden. Even though they were created good and in the image of God, and even though they had all of creation at their disposal, they chose to disobey God and ate fruit from the one tree in all of Paradise that was prohibited them. However you see this story—as simple myth or as some rendering of a historical reality—Adam and Eve's choice is repeated daily by millions of people, many of whom really aren't trying to be evil or to cause trouble. This story provides a strikingly accurate view of human nature. We regularly do what we know we shouldn't do; we consistently do not live up to our own plans or proceed in the way we envision ourselves living and acting. We repeatedly set our feet upon a good path, only to resist our own steps and cause all sorts of messes.

At the heart of our resistance is ego in its multiple forms. One way or the other, we put ourselves at the center of the universe. For some of us, that means we want to be in control of our own life; we don't want anyone telling us what to do or preventing us from doing whatever we want. We'll listen to advice, but we don't believe we really need help because we are smart and tough and self-sufficient.

Others of us want, ultimately, to be taken care of, to have our every need met and every desire fulfilled. Deep down we believe that we are entitled to this, and we act in quite unloving ways when our needs and desires get thwarted. Some of us want everybody to love and appreciate us. We constantly need to be recognized and adored. (I remember how I struggled, getting married to a man who already had children—some days I was so hurt and angry at not feeling like Number One in his life.)

And some of us must always feel significant and valuable. We push others to profess how important we are to them; we test people to see if they miss us enough when we're gone, or we get angry when we're not included in every discussion or decision. For this sort of person, major life changes can be hell, because she needs consistency: work that she performs well and for which she receives praise, and a stable group of people who make her feel validated and loved.

Whatever form our self-centeredness takes, it moves us to act not out of love but out of sheer need. If we need to be in control, then we push and use our power abusively. If we want to be taken care of, then we become needy and clingy, just to assure that someone will step up to the challenge. And if we must be loved and appreciated, we invent multiple ways to manipulate people into giving us what we want.

Some such attitude lies at the core of each of us. We don't want our own will to be thwarted. We want to protect ourselves from unpleasantness of every kind. We want comfort, control, freedom, pleasure. We want these things all the time. When we must give up any of them, even for a short time, it grates against our very being.

We want, really, to be our own gods. Which is why, throughout history, "God" has been presented to us so often as a monstrous projection of human nature: vengeful, egotistical, controlling, demanding, and always hungry for more. Even our sacred stories have not gone untouched by our ideas of what God should be like—just a bigger, stronger, unassailable version of us.

This drive to be god rather than to be in relationship with God is at the heart of all the sins we might care to name. The sad irony is this: all of our negative qualities arise out of our lack of relationship with God. If we give ourselves freely to this relationship, divine love will satisfy the soul so that we won't need to grasp after our flawed version of godlikeness. For instance, lust, envy, greed, and hatred are poor substitutes for the qualities that grow within us when we commune with God. Lust develops when we are unable to engage joyfully in the physical, sensual life we already have. Envy appears when, rather than accept who we are, we try to be somebody else. Greed grows when we refuse to develop gratitude for what we have and the generosity to share it. Hatred grows when we don't learn how to focus on life's beauty and potential for goodness. For every negative trait that, nurtured regularly, becomes a habit called sin, there is the trait we were meant to develop all along.

God's friendship, through the help of the Holy Spirit, teaches us how to nurture those traits and habits that lead to life. In the New Testament they are referred to as the fruit of the Spirit: "love, joy, peace, patience, kindness, generosity, faithfulness, gentleness, and self-control."[5]

It is easier to say no, God.
No requires no response, no plan.
No gives me time to make another excuse.
No avoids discomfort, discernment,
    discussion.
Just leave me alone with my no, all right?
It is my property, my prerogative,
my priority. It is mine. Yes.
That's what I like most about it.

Here in the Room 🍵

In previous chapters you have explored some of the things that can impede your progress toward friendship with God. But now concentrate on the Big Resistance, the resistance that persists in you no matter what, the resistance that urges you to say no to God's invitation. Use the list below to identify your problem points.

» How do you try to maintain control of your life?

» In what ways does your ego sometimes overcome your better impulses?

» How do you respond when others correct you or try to help you?

» What happens inside you when you aren't given proper credit, or when someone dismisses you as if you had nothing significant to offer?

» What is your general response toward authority figures?

» What do you most fear will be taken away from you if you say yes to God?

» What makes it difficult for you to ask for help?

» What makes it difficult for you to admit you're wrong?

» How do you respond to change—do you welcome it if it's good, or do you fight it regardless?

» How do you manipulate other people, and in what situations?

» How much time do you spend worrying over how much others love and appreciate you?

» What patterns of sin are rooted in your life: angry outbursts, manipulation of others, obsessive self-protection, and so on?

CHAPTER 17

Are you ready to be honest?

O LORD, you have searched me and known me.
You know when I sit down and when I rise up;
* you discern my thoughts from far away.*
You search out my path and my lying down,
* and are acquainted with all my ways.*
Even before a word is on my tongue,
* O LORD, you know it completely.*

Psalm 139:1–4

We've heard about John the Baptist, a wild kind of prophet who lived in the wilderness of Palestine. John ate locusts and wild honey and wore a camel's hair shirt. He told good people they needed to repent, to prepare them for the arrival of his cousin Jesus from Nazareth. He also told King Herod he needed to repent, since his illegal wife was already married to his brother. That's why the wife schemed with her daughter to have John beheaded—the exact request was that John's head be delivered on a platter. Royalty who misbehaved could not stay comfortable while the Baptist was around.

In spite of John's odd appearance and politically dangerous forthrightness, the Gospel of Mark notes that "people from the whole Judean countryside and all the people of Jerusalem were going out to him, and were baptized by him in the river Jordan, confessing their sins." *From the whole Judean countryside . . . all the people of Jerusalem.* I try to imagine what it would be like if even a tenth of the population in my city went to hear a single rock band or motivational speaker. It would make the world news.

Even more amazing, these people were not coming because John was making them feel good about themselves. He was "proclaiming a baptism of repentance for the forgiveness of sins." John was giving a name to the people's discontent; he was telling them the discomforting truth about themselves. Here was a whole countryside full of people who in the deepness of their souls understood that something was not right. Either they were not hearing this from their religious practitioners or they were so accustomed to their religion that they no longer heard what its teachers were saying. John's no-nonsense message woke them up to their spiritual need.

As you grow in awareness of God's presence, and as you become better acquainted with your own soul, you will notice that honesty in your life rises to a disconcerting level. While the culture around you says it's all right to play political games to get ahead, or to tell a few discreet lies, or to splurge regularly on yourself just because you can, you will know otherwise. When your soul is sending you signals that something is wrong but even good friends tell you not to worry so much and to give yourself a break, you will understand that something bigger is at stake. Spiritual awareness brings with it choices that sometimes only you will know about—those interior decisions that truly shape who you are.

Keep in mind that, not only do we as individuals resist movement toward God, but the whole of human society does as well. Rather than deal with wrongdoing, let's cover it up. Rather than ask the hard questions, let's hire better spin doctors. Rather than tell people what they don't want to know, tell them that everything's fine. Rather than demand that people change in order to heal and repair, tell them they're okay—in fact, they're wonderful and shouldn't let anything bother them, or they should take a pill so that things don't bother them so much. This social pressure to gloss over sin and its effects makes it difficult for a person to tell the truth even in private.

John the Baptist was not the first prophet to tell people the bad news they desperately needed to hear. Open the writings of any Old Testament prophet, such as Jeremiah or Ezekiel, and prepare to be shocked at the severity of their message. Don't be surprised at the reactions they received—derision, dismissal, persecution, imprisonment. Centuries later, Jesus lamented over Jerusalem as the city that killed its prophets. He could have been gazing over any American city today, or any human establishment anywhere.

What does it cost you to tell the truth? Does your marriage limp along while both of you keep on doing the same old things in the same ineffective ways? If you told the truth, there would probably be fights and tears and horrible pain—but then at least you could begin to deal with the problems.

Are you profoundly unhappy? And have you explored the possible causes of that unhappiness? If you learned what was wrong, then you'd need to act, wouldn't you? You would need to reconcile with a family member, or build a habit of prayer, or finally say no to some activities that are draining your energy but for which you receive praise.

Speaking of praise, whose approval are you trying to gain? Are you still trying to prove to your mother that you know how to run a household, or to some authority figure that you can be successful? Have you taken on too many responsibilities so you'll look better to certain peers whose credentials make you feel insignificant?

The people of Judea could not get enough of John the Baptist. He didn't tell them, "You're okay—and by doing steps one through five you will obtain all the success you dream of!" He said, "You're not okay, not at all. It's time to change your life. Turn around and go the right direction. Face the truth—and you will know God's mercy and forgiveness."

When it comes to spiritual progress, the bad news usually comes first. One day you step out the door and run right into the consequences of your unwise choices and your entangled heart. That's a hard moment, one that can last for weeks or months while you sort through the damage. But the last word is always the good word: God is already here, and you are already so completely loved that all of this mess will be just a little blip compared to what love can accomplish.

The Baptist is waiting for you, too. He wants to look into your eyes and say, "Things aren't going so well, are they?" You will find no condemnation in that face; he is deeply sad that you're in trouble. He's glad, though, to see your honesty come forth. He knows that healing will follow.

I waited a long time
and traveled many miles,
just to be told what I dreaded to hear:
You were wrong.
Darkness lives in you.
Your wound is ghastly.
After that,
I sat by a river for days.
The heat shimmered down,
and the insects sang,
and my tears dried up.
Then I got really mad—
at the waste, I mean, at how long
it took me to make the trip
and see the truth and follow it
out of that valley.
The first thing I had to do
was buy new shoes.

Here in the Room

Read this passage, and reread portions as you ponder the questions below.

> As [Jesus] and his disciples and a large crowd were leaving Jericho, Bartimaeus son of Timaeus, a blind beggar, was sitting by the roadside. When he heard that it was Jesus of Nazareth, he began to shout out and say, "Jesus, Son of David, have mercy on me!" Many sternly ordered him to be quiet, but he cried out even more loudly, "Son of David, have mercy on me!" Jesus stood still and said, "Call him here." And they called the blind man, saying to him, "Take heart; get up, he is calling you." So throwing off his cloak, he sprang up and came to Jesus. Then Jesus said to him, "What do you want me to do for you?" The blind man said to him, "My teacher, let me see again." Jesus said to him, "Go; your faith has made you well." Immediately he regained his sight and followed him on the way.
>
> —*Mark 10:46–52*

The blind man's need was obvious; why would Jesus ask him, "What do you want me to do for you?"

If Jesus passed through your town today and you went to see him, what would your obvious needs be?

Why do you think people tried to shush the blind man? Have others ever tried to silence your cries for help? If so, what did they do, and what do you think their motives were?

If Jesus were to ask you, "What do you want me to do for you," what would you say?

Reflect on how it feels to you to acknowledge that all is not well. Talk with God about your reaction.

CHAPTER 18

What does it mean to be converted?

> Create in me a clean heart, O God,
>> and put a new and right spirit within me.
> Do not cast me away from your presence,
>> and do not take your holy spirit from me.
> Restore to me the joy of your salvation,
>> and sustain in me a willing spirit.
>
> Psalm 51:10–12

I remember the day I said to God, "I hate you." I was thirty and had finally faced just how angry I was at the Almighty. I allowed myself to say the most awful things, the kinds of things for which God most certainly would have sent me straight to hell, had God been as small as some folks imagine. I remember also that, even as I cursed God, I knew I was really cursing god with a little g. I knew that the God Who Is lay beyond my perceptions and my anger. That fit of temper put me in a position to be converted.

We can spend decades, even a whole life, battling a phantom while thinking that we're fighting God. One of the most crucial aspects of conversion is giving up those false gods—the ones that are mere projections of the human ego. Only when we've given up our false gods can we turn and become friends with God. At the heart of conversion is the willingness to say yes—even if we have no accurate image of God—while we continue to struggle with the various aspects of our own resistance.

God invites us into the Room. When we dare say yes and come in, that is conversion. When we decide that, yet again, we will not enter "this time," we are acting out of resistance, and this is our sin, to say no and to keep saying no. Much of our resistance will lose its power when our friendship with God is allowed to develop. When we enter the Room and open ourselves to God's attention, we are increasingly able to overcome the damage we've accrued and to move beyond history and falsehood.

How do we experience conversion, a change of heart? Is it something that happens only to horrible people who decide one day to reform, to change from being God's enemy to becoming God's friend? Or does each person—regardless of that person's level of good and evil—need to make a change of heart or direction in order to encounter the God who created us and desires our company?

We have heard and read the stories of great conversions— the murderer who finds God and turns his life around entirely; the adulteress who is overwhelmed by the love and forgiveness of Jesus, and thus leaves her life for a better one. Most conversions, though, are not 180 degrees. Some are just a few degrees on a given day. The misconception about conversion is that it happens once and is a grand, dramatic affair. The typical conversion is one of many over a lifetime. By degrees we turn to God. We choose, day after day and year after year, to enter the Room and dwell with God and be changed. We also choose, day after day and year after year, to leave the Room and to ignore it or avoid it. Our friendship with God can run hot and cold, depending on our circumstances, our self-awareness, and our individual spiritual battles.

The faith communities of my childhood believed in a once-for-all conversion. If you could not pinpoint the day and hour in which you gave your life to Jesus, there was some question as to whether you were truly a "born-again" Christian. Every conversion needed that Saul-of-Tarsus quality, the drama of a before-and-after transformation.

Of course, even Saul (better known as Paul) continued to be converted; his letters in the New Testament are vivid chronicles of a man, and of the communities he helped, learning day by day what it meant to follow Jesus, to love and serve God.

In real life, even those "born-again" converts underwent numerous conversions. In such faith communities, conversions that happened after the initial one were called "rededications." When I was growing up, I rededicated my life to Christ at least twice a year (usually during spring and fall revival services). I renewed my commitment to follow Jesus and to grow into the person God had created me to be. Our religious leaders didn't bat an eye when we marched up the aisle multiple times—to rededicate our lives, to repent of sin that had overcome us, to say yes to something new God was calling us to do. All of these moments were conversions folded into a lifelong conversion called faith.

Resistance of all sorts will re-emerge throughout life, even after major conversion, after years of friendship with God. We will always deal with some form of resistance. On some days it will be present in an old fear that just won't die; on other days, our resistance will be a full-blown fit of ego, when we refuse God's invitation and even take pride in the fact that we've done so with such power and self-possession.

And because of the ever-present resistance, we will need to develop the ever-present willingness to say yes to God—yes to help, yes to forgiveness, yes to learning something new, yes to being overwhelmed by love.

I was minding my own business, really.
But that day something opened, like a door,
or my heart, as if Someone had walked into
the room and was simply there.
At that point it's useless to pretend
that you're alone or that you don't care,
or that your soul doesn't feel as if
it's breaking in two.
It's useless to write some softer version,
because Someone is right here,
and you will never, ever be the same.
Your self has opened, and Love roams
your rooms and even if you kick it out
because you're afraid or stupid
or whatever—even if you say, "Leave!"
you know that having felt the Presence

you will ever after be desperate without it.
Once Someone walks into the room,
that face stays with you—that,
and the voice that resonates
in your bones, your blood, your everything.

Here in the Room

We turn now to some traditional prayers of confession. For centuries, these prayers have helped people name and describe their resistance toward God. Spend time with these prayers before reading further.

> Most merciful God,
> we confess that we have sinned against you
> in thought, word, and deed,
> by what we have done,
> and by what we have left undone.
> We have not loved you with our whole heart;
> we have not loved our neighbors as ourselves.
> We are truly sorry and we humbly repent.
> For the sake of your Son Jesus Christ,
> have mercy on us and forgive us;
> that we may delight in your will,
> and walk in your ways,
> to the glory of your Name. Amen
>
> —*The Book of Common Prayer*

Lord, my earthly nature is stood before my eyes like a
barren field, which has few good plants grown in it.
Alas, sweetest Jesus and Christ,
now send me the sweet rain of your humanity
and the hot sun of your living Godhead
and the gentle dew of the Holy Spirit
that I may wail and cry out the aches of my heart.

—*Mechtild of Magdeburg*[6]

Have mercy on me, O God,
according to your steadfast love;
according to your abundant mercy
blot out my transgressions.
Wash me thoroughly from my iniquity,
and cleanse me from my sin.

—*Psalm 51:1–2*

What phrases from these prayers resonate for you?
Which phrases best describe the way you feel?
Which phrases are troublesome for you, and why?

Your own "conversion" . . .

Tell the story of a time when you turned and began walking in a
different direction. That story may include several distinct turning points, or you may identify only one or two moments when
you turned intentionally away from being god and toward God.

In what ways have you experienced your own sense of sin? How does resistance tend to crop up in your daily life?

What does *repentance* mean to you? How have you experienced it?

Compose your own prayer of confession. Write it however you like, borrowing phrases from other prayers or creating something completely yours.

If you want to be a little daring . . .
Although you have been in the Room with God, imagine that you are entering it all over again. And you are carrying your written confession.

Sit down, or lie down, or stand, or bow in God's presence, and read your confession as a prayer.

How does God respond to your confession?

CHAPTER 19

How do you get in your own way?

I will study the way that is blameless.

. . .

I will walk with integrity of heart
within my house;
I will not set before my eyes
anything that is base.

. . .

Perverseness of heart shall be far from me;
I will know nothing of evil.

Psalm 101:2–4

Wrhen I was in my twenties, I shared with a good friend that I felt the Holy Spirit leading me to take better care of myself. This care included paying better attention to my appearance. I had never considered myself physically attractive, and at some level I had decided not to bother with makeup or nice clothes or hairstyles—what was the point? But now I was feeling nudged in a new direction, and whether or not I felt pretty was beside the point. I needed to develop habits of simple self-respect, and I needed to acknowledge that my physical appearance was intricately connected to the part of me who composed music and studied the Bible.

When I explained this to my friend, she laughed a little and said that the Holy Spirit was leading her in the opposite direction. She had always been attractive. From early adolescence she had spent hours every week working on her makeup and hair, and she was particular about her clothes. But now she was being nudged in a new direction. She needed to play down her looks and learn to be content without so much attention to the outward person. All through school she had been distracted by guys bothering her, and—this seemed unbelievable to me!—her self-image had suffered from all the harassment. She and I had a lot in common, but our needs in this area were different. If I kept neglecting my physical self, the person I would project to others would give them reason to think less of me, to ignore or even disrespect me. My friend, on the other hand, would attract undue attention if she continued giving the physical self such high priority.

We must learn to understand what hurts us and what helps us. And often what we identify as hurtful cannot clearly be labeled as sin. I never considered the use or nonuse of makeup to endanger my soul in any way. But the Holy Spirit helped me recognize that my aversion to makeup was rooted in a self-perception that had to change—just as my friend recognized that in order for her to concentrate more on things that really mattered, she needed to become less conspicuous. She continued to take care of herself, but her emphasis changed.

Sometimes our resistance toward God and toward our own well-being is not so obvious; it's hidden within attitudes and personal habits that we form in order to protect ourselves or to help us feel significant. These attitudes and habits distance us from others and from the Divine, and they enable us to keep dealing with life in ways that aren't working for us.

What hurts your progress in life? What gets in the way of your growing relationship with God and others? Perhaps you hold back from conversations because you grew up believing you had nothing important to contribute. Or maybe you're one of those people who must be given permission for everything—you have so little confidence in your own gifts, desires, and intuition that you're always waiting for someone else to tell you what to do. Yet God has so much for you to do in the world, and sometimes it's something only you can do, and it's something no one else would ever think of or see as valuable. No one will give you permission to go forward, so there you'll be, stuck and unfulfilled.

Perhaps you've developed the habit of hanging around people who aren't good for you. I'm not talking about thieves or drug dealers but about people who simply drag you down. Some people have a way of making you doubt yourself, or they fill up your time with useless talk and emotional venting. Or they're always pulling you in directions you don't want to go—to spend too much money or look at life negatively or escape your responsibilities. Or they suck you dry with their neediness and their own lack of purpose or direction. Please remember that just because a person needs someone, that someone may not always be you. Sorting out relationships requires ongoing discernment.

When I facilitate a writers' workshop, I make the point repeatedly that most of what we call writing is, besides simply learning the craft, learning our own creative process so that we can work with it rather than against it. As a writer I must learn what frees me to be creative, what disrupts my energy, what leads me to burnout, and what helps me stay disciplined when the going is rough. These factors are different for each of us, and thus the creative life requires self-awareness, self-respect, and self-trust.

The same is true for the spiritual life. Certain things inspire us, while other things discourage us. Some people build us up, and others tear us down (even if they don't intend to). We hold some self-perceptions that help us embrace our gifts and dreams, while we hang on to others that cause us to doubt our worth and second-guess our every decision.

Some of my habits are good for me, such as walking when I need to think or pray. Other habits will not be so good for me in the long run, such as comforting my weariness or sadness with foods that are full of fat and calories. In fact, if I'm not careful, I'll find something *every single day* that calls for comfort, sometimes *twice* a day. And before I know it I'm downing several cappuccinos or gourmet hot chocolates in a week, and the sugar is making me crash harder than ever, yet the caffeine is preventing me from sleeping well. This is a somewhat trivial example, but if I can learn to recognize this as a not-so-helpful habit, then perhaps I can face honestly some of the more damaging ones.

For instance, there are days, even weeks, when I redirect my general frustration by blaming every inconvenience or mishap on my husband—he didn't think ahead, or he didn't keep track of something, or he didn't do some household task the way I would. I usually don't tell him that I blame him; I merely do it inwardly—and then deny it later when he asks me why I'm mad at him. Repeating this hurtful pattern is easier than admitting that life was never designed solely so that I would have one perfect day after another. Most days have their quota of frustrations and mishaps, and if I'm a grown-up I learn to take them in stride. But it's much easier to blame my husband than to grow up. This is not good for anyone. I could listen to the Holy Spirit, who reminds me that I am not the center of the universe and that I am not loving my husband when I develop such a vindictive attitude toward him. I could listen, but that would challenge a well-practiced habit.

Jesus gave a whole sermon on the difference between simply keeping the letter of the law and internalizing the spirit of the law. He said, of course it's wrong to kill—but you kill every time you entertain hateful thoughts and feelings toward other people. Of course it's wrong to commit adultery, but do you understand the damage you cause to your own soul when you simply fantasize about someone else's spouse?

God provided laws and Scripture and faith traditions to help us find our way. In addition, God has written those laws in our hearts. God has placed within us the wisdom to understand—in detail and nuance that Scripture cannot really provide—what harms us and what keeps us from enjoying intimate friendship with the Divine.

I could say simply that I have poor instincts;
I don't really know what's good for me.
And maybe this is true; maybe television
and poor diet have conditioned me
to ignore my own true thoughts,
my own sensible body. Maybe I am really
very wise already; maybe inside me
there is a robust and healthy woman
who has learned how to stop
hitting herself in the head again and again,
who doesn't keep tripping over herself
because she is always in the way.

Here in the Room ☕ _____

Say a prayer that goes something like this: God, I want to stop getting in the way of my own progress. I know you have placed within me the spiritual intuition to discern what hurts me and what helps me. Please help me connect with that wisdom. And once I figure things out, help me take action.

In the days that follow, make two lists: 1) What hurts me? 2) What helps me?

If you want to be a little daring . . .

Ask God to show you two people who care about you and who would be willing to explore with you the following questions:

> » How do I most often get in my own way?
> » How do you see me being good to myself?
> » How do you see me not being so good to myself?

When you feel ready, approach these people and work on the questions together. Be sure to ask for clarification if you don't understand what they tell you. Ask them to give you examples of what they're talking about. The people who love you enough to be honest with you about this topic can give you startling insight. And because they love you, they can give you the bad news in a way that's gentle enough to receive.

CHAPTER 20

How will forgiveness change you?

Happy are those whose transgression is
  forgiven,
 whose sin is covered.
Happy are those to whom the LORD imputes
  no iniquity,
 and in whose spirit there is no deceit.

Psalm 32:1–2

Watch a group of children working on an art project, and
before long you will see different behaviors emerge. Some
children will use the project as yet one more excuse to have fun,
to explore, and to be as creative as they like. The other group
will go about it much more seriously, will get frustrated easily,
and will then worry that the final result won't be good enough.
To some extent, these differences can be explained by natural
temperament. But you can be sure that the level of freedom

expressed by these children is also related to their experience of forgiveness.

The child who experiences primarily judgment and punishment—at home, in school, in church or neighborhood—will not be free in anything she does. She will get upset at every mistake, and she will worry that the end result will bring anger or ridicule. And she definitely won't experiment—no, she will ask the teacher repeatedly what the rules are and ask if she's "doing it right."

The child who experiences acceptance and forgiveness will be free to make mistakes, try something new, play as she works, and even enjoy what the other kids are making.

Those children will grow up and eventually have children of their own. The one who learned judgment will worry over her kids and turn them toward worry, toward anxiety about failure and doing everything right. The parent who learned forgiveness will help create an atmosphere in which her children can discover who they truly are and become the gifted people they are meant to be.

Yes, forgiveness is pivotal to how we get along in the world. Without it, we will never be free. With it, we live in freedom and also free others to live well.

Once again, we must confront our perceptions of God. Is God always waiting for us to screw up? And when we do, how does God treat us? And once we've made a mess of things, do God's expectations of us change, and does God's opinion of us change? And when we keep messing up, is God happy to see us, or do we feel that it's best to just stay away for a while—to avoid church and stop trying to pray and stay away from people who do?

It might help to ask different questions:

If God is always waiting for us to mess up and looks forward to punishing us, then why does God offer a solution at all? Why send prophets and visionaries to warn us away from the trouble we're about to bring upon ourselves? Why send John the Baptist, or Jesus, to tell of a better way?

If God expects very little of us, then who was Jesus talking to when he delivered the Sermon on the Mount, in which he described a way to live so virtuous ("Love your enemies. . . . Don't worry about what you'll eat or drink") that it seems impossible to accomplish? Why put such a challenge in front of us if there is no divine intention to help us meet that challenge?

Many of us tend to think of forgiveness as God's grudging willingness not to destroy us, even though we are failures. But forgiveness is more like a door God has opened so that we can walk through and find the restoration we need. When we are able to change our ideas about forgiveness to such an extent that we see the open door and God's great smile inviting us in, we will live in a new and freer way.

Now that I know you're not angry,
everything feels possible:
I can grow and change
and learn and try again.
In fact, what is there to stop me?
Maybe it's childish to think
that God is on my side,
but I remember how impossible it was
to get through a day when I feared
that nothing would go well ever again,
when I was sure that you saw me
as multiple failures just waiting to happen,
some poor soul you had to save.
But no—you embrace me, enjoy me;
you wait for all my glory to shine through.
The saving was all about drawing me back
into that togetherness, that glory-making
with you always close,
with me tucked up against your heart.

Here in the Room

Read this passage to prepare for the meditation that follows.

One of the Pharisees asked Jesus to eat with him, and he went into the Pharisee's house and took his place at the table. And a woman in the city, who was a sinner, having learned that he was eating in the Pharisee's house, brought an alabaster jar of ointment. She stood behind him at his feet, weeping, and began to bathe his feet with her tears and to dry them with her hair. Then she continued kissing his feet and anointing them with the ointment. Now when the Pharisee . . . saw it, he said to himself, "If this man were a prophet, he would have known who and what kind of woman this is who is touching him." . . . Jesus spoke up and said to him, . . . "A certain creditor had two debtors; one owed five hundred denarii, and the other fifty. When they could not pay, he canceled the debts for both of them. Now which of them will love him more?" Simon answered, "I suppose the one for whom he canceled the greater debt." And Jesus said to him, "You have judged rightly." Then turning toward the woman, he said to Simon, "Do you see this woman? I entered your house; you gave me no water for my feet, but she has bathed my feet with her tears and dried them with her hair. You gave me no kiss, but from the time I came in she has not stopped kissing my feet. You did not anoint my head with oil,

but she has anointed my feet with ointment.* Therefore,
I tell you, her sins, which were many, have been forgiven; hence she has shown great love. But the one to
whom little is forgiven loves little." Then he said to her,
"Your sins are forgiven. . . . Your faith has saved you; go
in peace."

—*Luke 7:36–50*

Get comfortable, quiet your mind, and enter this
meditation:

*You are the woman in this story. You heard others talking about
Jesus and finally went to hear him for yourself. His stunning dec-
larations of God's love shattered your defenses, and you have spent
days weeping and praying. You have gone back to your mother, your
father, and every person you pushed away through the years. There
was the friend you betrayed, the man you loved and left. There was
the child you aborted and the other child you didn't love enough.
There were the people you used for safety, for help with your crises,
and then forgot about. There were the others who needed you but
whom you were too busy to help. And don't forget all the abuse you
heaped upon yourself—the destructive entanglements and transient
lovers, the financial debts and neglect of your health, the lies and
temper tantrums.*

---

* Washing the feet of a guest and kissing that guest in greeting were common courtesies in that culture. Anointing with oil would have suggested
that Simon considered Jesus a great teacher or one appointed by God.

All of this is piled up around you, like mounds of debris. This is who you have become through life's cruel chance and your own poor choices. And you were willing to accept that responsibility, never expecting help from anybody. In fact, you grew to expect not much at all—life was hard, and so were you.

But then came this person who could see through all that debris. He stood there and smiled and welcomed you and all the other people known as failures. He said that God's forgiveness was endless, that God's love was right here, just for you. You tried not to listen, but later those words repeated in your mind. And you had to see if this man was for real. So you pushed past everyone to get into this nice, decent home, and you endured the remarks and the hateful looks of everybody just to get to him. You expected that when you got close, he'd change his tune. He'd see you for what you really are, and, looking uncomfortable, would send you away as soon as he could.

But he was thrilled to meet you! He didn't draw back when you took his feet in your hands—and he took your face in his. He said, "Your sins are forgiven"—just like that. Then, "Your faith has saved you; go in peace." His eyes and voice said exactly the same thing: Everything is all right. You are not a prisoner of your history, because nothing can get between you and God's love.

Write your response to this experience.

PART FIVE

Conversation

One day I was in the bathroom, standing at the basin, washing my hands. And Jesus was there. In the bathroom with me. Telling me without words that it was all right and there was work for me to do. I did not question his presence. It seemed very strange and embarrassing to me that he would approach me in the bathroom because I was a private and rather prudish child. Why didn't he come to me in church? Or when I was saying my prayers? Or even in the park? . . . Certainly I didn't tell anybody. I have never mentioned it before in all these years. But I didn't forget.

MADELEINE L'ENGLE, *BRIGHT EVENING STAR*[7]

I have never considered myself good at prayer. I have started and stopped countless methods for making prayer a strong habit in my life. As a younger person I prayed differently from how I pray now, and I think this is progress, but I still don't feel very effective when it comes to this aspect of my friendship with God.

What we must remember about prayer is that it is conversation, and conversation changes because people do. Conversation also shifts and adjusts depending on who is participating. You speak differently with your mother than with a close friend. You probably speak differently with men than with women, although the difference is subtle and possibly unconscious on your part. Some days you're talkative, and other days you just want to be left alone. And, we hope, your conversation now is much deeper, wiser, and better integrated with your real experience than when you were younger. You continue to learn how to express yourself with more clarity, honesty, and compassion. Best of all, the years have taught you to be a better listener.

CHAPTER 21

What has prayer been for you?

The LORD answer you in the day of trouble!
  The name of the God of Jacob protect you!
May he send you help from the sanctuary,
  and give you support from Zion.
May he remember all your offerings,
  and regard with favor your burnt sacrifices.
May he grant you your heart's desire,
  and fulfill all your plans.

Psalm 20:1–4

I have used Psalms throughout these chapters because they reveal the details of human longing, emotion, frailty, and mindset. The psalmist doesn't hold back, and it's a relief to see that I'm not the only one who is impatient with God's silence or who sometimes wants my enemies to suffer. The psalms are exquisite poetry of devotion—on its good days and its bad days.

However, during the adolescent, formative years of my faith, I fell under the influence of people who didn't recognize that the Psalms were poetic expression but who took them quite literally. When the psalmist said, "May he grant you your heart's desire, and fulfill all your plans," that was interpreted to be a promise from God. I'm sure that many Christians in my life did not take such a simplistic approach, but usually the more literalistic believers are also the noisiest and pushiest (and often they have their own television broadcasts). The sad result was that, very gradually and subtly, I grew more and more disappointed with God. I was not finding my heart's desire, and my plans kept getting thwarted. I would pray for what I desired in life, but when nothing happened I had to conclude that either I didn't have enough faith (a common view in some Christian circles) or that God was reneging on a deal. This absorption of bad theology, coupled with ego-driven prayer, did much damage to my conversation with God.

You may or may not have "prayer baggage," but you probably have some history with prayer that continues to shape your approach to it now. If your background is Catholic or some other liturgical tradition, then you likely memorized several different prayers as a child, and those prayers still bubble up from memory when you attend church or feel a need to connect with God in the course of a workday.

I attended church with my Methodist grandmother when I was very young, and along with the other kids I cycled through the Sunday school class she taught, memorizing the Lord's Prayer, the Apostles' Creed, the Beatitudes, and the Ten

Commandments. During those years, prayers were small, portable comforts, words I could hold close and repeat whenever I needed them. This isn't a bad introduction to prayer. When we're children we learn to talk by mimicking what others say. When we grow up, it's time to form our own thoughts and put words to them.

I experienced a genuine conversion when I was about eleven, during a revival. I had finally named, in front of many witnesses, my desire for God. Here was an excruciating kind of joy as my soul opened to grace and I graduated from a comfortable, habit-formed spirituality to a faith much more intentional. A couple of years later, I joined the Baptist church, and for at least the next decade my prayer life was shaped by country preachers and their congregations. In that faith community I learned that prayer was passionate speech directed toward a heavenly Father. It was spiritual commitment fused with emotion. It was a form of expressing love to others, asking God that this cancer be healed and that a young father find employment, for one evil government to be toppled and for another king or prime minister to heed God's voice. Prayer was a critical part of the community's expression, requests spoken aloud in a music-charged room while others added their assent with "amen" or "yes, Lord."

Certain protocols were assumed in a life of faithful prayer. Praise must precede anything else; praise was a way to greet God. After that, thanksgiving for our many blessings. Then confession of our sins, to clear away whatever might be standing between us and God. Then intercession—prayer for others. Last of all, petition—prayer for the self. Communal prayers during worship services consisted primarily of intercession; as a congregation we handed God our list of needs. And because people were usually unwilling to make public their more personal needs, the only requests verbalized during communal prayer were for healing and sometimes for money. So we went down the list of people in the hospital or scheduled for surgery or diagnosed with a disease. I never once heard a request for God to heal someone's struggling marriage or help them overcome their bad temper or overeating or argumentativeness or sloppy money management. Somehow our communal prayer was not representative of what we were told personal prayer should be. For instance, I never heard a preacher confess to God the sins of the church (racism, sexism, neglect of the poor, and so on), yet I was instructed to confess my sins specifically before requesting any help from God.

During my teens, I became involved with some zealous pray-ers who gave more explicit instruction for talking to the Almighty. If I wanted something, I should "claim it in Jesus' name," which was the ultimate formula for prayer success. Moreover, I should be as specific as possible, so that God could answer me specifically. God was the king with all sorts of riches. He was waiting for me to ask so that he could give them to me.

Other members of the Christian family have their own ways of skewing, codifying, and oversimplifying prayer, but I will leave the telling of those stories to the people who have lived them. The point is this: If we linger long in that sort of mindset, then prayer becomes a means of meeting our needs, and little else. God becomes a stern king with goodies to pass out if only we ask in the right way. Prayer is a to-do list and a human strategy for trying to manipulate God.

such misguided desires. Thank you
for staying so close while I screamed
in another direction entirely.

Here in the Room

What prayer baggage do you have?

How, and when, and from whom, did you learn to pray? What did others teach you about prayer through the way they prayed?

What has always bothered or perplexed you about prayer?

Write your own definition of prayer:

Talk with God about the responses you've just written.

CHAPTER 22

How do you bring your whole self to prayer?

I give you thanks, O LORD, with my
*   whole heart;*
* before the gods I sing your praise;*
I bow down toward your holy temple
* and give thanks to your name for your*
*   steadfast love and your faithfulness*

. . .

On the day I called, you answered me,
* you increased my strength of soul.*

Psalm 138:1–3

Not long ago, I went on an eight-day Ignatian retreat, a week set aside for focused prayer. I took my laptop because I type quickly and find it easier to journal on computer than in longhand. As I moved into the retreat, I kept glancing at the laptop but didn't feel that using it would be the best way to spend the time. I'm a writer, and once I begin writing, my words take on their own life, and I get carried off on my ideas. My sense was that getting carried away with words would not accommodate my conversation with God.

What I ended up doing all week was drawing pictures. Because I have no ability in this area, I was under no pressure to do it well. The drawing enabled me to slow down my thoughts, really dwell with phrases and images, and let the Holy Spirit speak. I didn't even unpack the laptop; I needed to bring other aspects of myself into the prayer process. The word-person needed to play with colored pencils for a few days. The prayer I experienced during that time still reverberates in my daily thinking and doing—in fact, that week of prayer did much to inform the writing of this book.

In 2007, Paraclete Press published a book by Sybil MacBeth, *Praying in Color: Drawing a New Path to God.*[8] The author's own deep need to pray—and an elusive connection to more traditional prayer—compelled her into a mode of conversation with God that involved drawing shapes to represent the people she prayed for and then praying by adding colors, more shapes, and words. This book is revolutionizing prayer for many people today. It's an excellent example of bringing the intuitive part of the self to God.

In the affluent and educated West, we're pretty good at bringing our minds to prayer. We can sit and think and express ourselves to our particular mental concept of God. When we are in distress, we might allow our emotions to enter prayer; it is considered appropriate to cry while praying, although people around us will grow uncomfortable if we wail or sob extensively.

But stop and consider: what is involved when you converse with a good friend? I'm talking about the friend who demands always, in a loving way, that you be honest, that you bravely go forward when the time is right, no matter what threatens to get in your way. This friend is able to bear your anger or sorrow when you need to express it. This friend reminds you of the good things in your life and of the good work you have done. This friend recognizes your gifts and appreciates the nooks and crannies of your personality and your life history. This friend is someone with whom you can be your whole self.

When you have a conversation with a friend like that, you can express yourself fully and honestly without fear of rejection or judgment. You can even throw a tantrum sometimes, knowing that your friend will listen, wait for you to calm down, and then say the right thing or just sit with you. In this sort of conversation you speak with your eyes, your facial expression, your tone of voice, and your gestures. You form sentences out of what you're going through, putting into words your emotions as well as your thoughts. You speak freely of deeply spiritual matters, whether or not you have figured out what they mean or what you must do about them.

In this sort of conversation, you are free to talk, laugh, shout, and cry. You are also free to sit and say nothing. And—this is important—you often don't say anything at all but listen attentively to what your friend is saying. And sometimes no one needs to speak.

We can learn to talk with God in the same way. We express happiness at what has gone well today and anxiety about what might not go well tomorrow. We bring our weariness and our tears. Perhaps we gust out a days' worth of frustration, or we have a good laugh. Sometimes the Holy Spirit helps us see how ridiculous is our worry or irritation, and this can help us move beyond it.

We also bring our physical selves to prayer. Whether we kneel in private or participate in a group dance during a worship service, we can bring the whole body into our prayer. When we express with the body what we are experiencing in the soul, we live as people who are integrated rather than compartmentalized. We can borrow wisdom from the East and incorporate something as simple as the yoga pose for sun salutation, which opens the body upward to greet what is greater than the self. Yoga, Tai Chi, and other systems of body practice help us meditate with our bodies, becoming more aware of muscles, joints, and skin and how they respond to what's going on at this moment.

Many people walk as they pray; the easy rhythm of their steps helps them move into a spiritual rhythm. At several retreat centers where I present workshops, I've had opportunities to walk the stations of the cross. An increasing number of retreat houses have permanent labyrinths, and I walk these as well. A labyrinth can be walked in whatever speed and style you want. There are set ways to pray and meditate using a labyrinth—just as there are various devotions to accompany walking the stations— or you can create your own mode of prayer as you go. Christians have used both of these "walking prayer" forms for centuries, so they are certainly worth trying today. In fact, today's frantic pace of living makes these practices even more important to our spiritual health.

We can pray through our breathing, exhaling our fear, anger, and anxiety and inhaling peace, gratitude, and wisdom. We can exhale confession and inhale thanksgiving. This sort of prayer becomes particularly meaningful when we remember that our bodies have been breathing since our birth, whether we're awake or asleep, whether we notice or not. The fact that you and I breathe, one moment to the next, through hours, days, and year upon year, is nothing less than miraculous. And so to spend a few moments paying attention to our breathing, and thanking God for that breath, is as real as prayer gets.

The point of exploring different ways to pray is to become more comfortable with all aspects of the self and bring them to God. A variety of prayer methods can bring balance. If I'm more of a thinker-type, it's good for me to learn how to engage my emotions and my body in prayer. If I'm emotive already—frequently crying while in prayer and able to feel ecstatic and joyous—then I might use liturgical prayer sometimes, which will give my prayer more structure and take my mind through ideas and thoughts that I wouldn't approach on my own. After decades of praying in churches where only spontaneous prayer was used, I was relieved to find a denomination that used primarily a written liturgy—finally the pressure was off to create, on the spot, well-crafted prayers spoken aloud. I could simply pray the prayers Christians have prayed for centuries, bringing my mind and heart into accordance with those thoughts and rhythms.

When I spend time with a friend, I want that person's *presence.* After a while, a phone call or an e-mail just isn't good enough—I want a body to hug, a face to gaze upon, the whole person behind the phone voice and written words. God wants our whole presence, not just our thoughts flung heavenward when we have a second and not just our emotional overflow when the day has gone sour. Prayer is the sharing of presence.

Can I sigh loudly?
Can I sing a song I really like?
Can I lie down and stretch my back?
Can I bury my face in a pillow?
Can I recite a poem?
Can I draw pictures of oceans and birds?
Can I use a little rhythm?
Can I borrow lovely phrases from
someone who died long ago?
Can I refrain from speaking?
Can I sit here and watch the light move?
Can I raise my arms and hope a little?
Yes, and yes, and . . . always your
answer is yes—*and* please come.

Here in the Room

Can you remember specific prayer experiences as being powerful, or profound? If so, what happened, and why do you think those experiences were so memorable?

How are emotions involved in your prayer? Can you express them, or do you repress them, especially anger and hurt?

How does your physical self relate to your conversation with God? How aware are you of what your body is doing when you pray? How have you involved your body in prayer?

Do you ever sing when you pray? Have you tried drawing pictures or coloring? How might you do prayer more visually?

Get into a comfortable position. Take several slow, deep breaths. Now, close your eyes and be silent for a few moments. If worries intrude or you keep thinking of things you need to do, write them down and set them aside and go back to a quiet mind.

And then imagine yourself in prayer. Imagine what you look like; see yourself walking to a specific place and praying there. Observe what you do with your body while praying. Note the expression on your face. Listen to the words of prayer that come out of your mouth—or, if you are praying silently, hear the unspoken thoughts.

When the prayer in your imagination is finished, reflect on what you witnessed. Write down your observations. Talk with God about them.

CHAPTER 23

Where is the Holy Spirit in this conversation?

But you, O LORD, are a shield around me,
my glory, and the one who lifts up my head.
I cry aloud to the LORD,
and he answers me from his holy hill.

Psalm 3:3–4

I once heard a great description of prayer. A husband and wife come home from their respective long and frustrating workdays and sit down to the evening meal. Burdened with multiple concerns, the man lets out a heavy sigh. The woman's eyes get misty, because she understands and shares her husband's discouragement. They say their regular mealtime prayer, but in reality they have prayed already. His sigh went straight to heaven, and her tears have spoken what can't be translated into words.

The Spirit helps us in our weakness; for we do not know how to pray as we ought, but that very Spirit intercedes with sighs too deep for words. And God, who searches the heart, knows what is the mind of the Spirit, because the Spirit intercedes for the saints according to the will of God.

—Romans 8:26–27

Jesus called the Holy Spirit our Advocate, or helper. We are responsible to do what we know to do in this unpredictable process called the spiritual life. But our knowledge and our perceptions are limited, and we need help. The Holy Spirit's ongoing work is to help us, whether we are working or making decisions or praying. Chapter 33 of this book explores how the Spirit engages with us in daily life. For now, let's consider how the Holy Spirit joins in the conversation called prayer.

Have you ever been in a conversation with someone who apparently has forgotten most of what you said in a previous one? You wonder if you dreamed the prior conversation or if you really were so unclear that this person seemingly has no clue about what you said. Memory enables a conversation to go forward, and the Holy Spirit helps us remember what we already know about our life of faith. Sometimes we recall something from a homily or a phrase from Scripture. Sometimes we remember something from a conversation we had years ago. Sometimes we recall an event in real life or in a dream.

The Holy Spirit's participation with us involves a constant gathering and regathering of our many stories. Much of what the Old Testament prophets (who were said to be "filled" with the Holy Spirit) did for the nation Israel was to remind the people of how God had already participated in their history. Human beings have a great capacity for remembering, but we neglect that capacity, especially when forgetfulness suits our laziness or resistance. Thus the Holy Spirit helps our memory and awareness.

As women, we might well relate to this aspect of the Holy Spirit's participation, because many of us have been the story keepers in our families. Often it's the women who keep the scrapbooks and photo albums, the mementos and souvenirs, the memory of important moments and funny anecdotes. We keep track of and sort through all the little pieces of life, both for ourselves and our loved ones. I like to think the Holy Spirit expresses one of the feminine aspects of the Divine in this work of remembering and keeping.

According to Christian belief, the Holy Spirit dwells within us.

> *What human being knows what is truly human except the human spirit that is within? So also no one comprehends what is truly God's except the Spirit of God. Now we have received not the spirit of the world, but the Spirit that is from God, so that we may understand the gifts bestowed on us by God. And we speak of these things in words not taught by human wisdom but taught by the Spirit, interpreting spiritual things to those who are spiritual.*
>
> —*1 Corinthians 2:11–13*

What this means is that our human life indeed merges with divine life, and our prayer grows out of that merging. We are *in community* with God, and our very sighs and tears, our hopes and desires, are all constantly being expressed to God Who Is.

The Holy Spirit's contribution to our conversation with God is often our deeper sensitivity and our intuitive wisdom.

> I will pour out my spirit on all flesh;
> your sons and your daughters shall prophesy,
>   your old men shall dream dreams,
>   and your young men shall see visions.
>
> —Joel 2:28

God was present in Jesus as a physical person who could accompany people and teach them directly, allowing them to experience firsthand God's response to them. God is present in the Holy Spirit as a spiritual person who offers wisdom, comfort, faith, and companionship. In dwelling with us, the Holy Spirit can speak through our own emotions, memories, thoughts, dreams, and desires. And so we are able to converse with God, because God in us is talking with God over all and in all.

This doesn't mean that our every feeling and thought is inspired or in harmony with God. But it does mean that we can enter prayer with openness and hope, trusting in divine love to both assist our prayers and respond to them. Maybe we really want this new job, or really want to buy that house. But the job or the sale could fall through. So we bring those desires to God in prayer and say, "Lord, I really want this, but I can't see the future, and for all I know, this wouldn't be the best outcome.

So, please, may the best thing happen. And help me go with the flow. Help me trust that everything will be all right."

In prayer, we can learn not to grasp and not to demand. When we take a desire to God, we acknowledge that it may also be God's desire; but we also acknowledge that even good desires do not always take us where we need to go. And so the Holy Spirit helps us loosen our grip on the situation as we offer it to God in prayer.

The Holy Spirit also helps us to become more involved in what God is already doing in the world. God is always at work; the Holy Spirit keeps us aware of that. In prayer, we learn to be still and to listen to God's desires for us and for the world.

It is a good idea to include Scripture reading in our prayer. Scripture—written under the inspiration of the Holy Spirit— reminds us of how God is active in the universe, through mercy and peacemaking, through caring for the poor, through our taking pleasure in the gifts of others. And as we meditate on Scripture, we listen to God's part of the conversation. We are reminded of what is ultimately important, trusting the Holy Spirit to bring certain ideas or issues to the front of our attention. In this way, prayer allows us to participate in a divine process that is much larger than we are.

One day I remembered a few little words
that got to the heart of my worry.
I didn't recall who said them to me
or why—but I was happy
for their return on the wave of years
to land in such a helpful place.
Another time, I was trying hard
to better myself, you know,
the kind of trying that is desperate
but well intentioned.
And a kind woman way down
in my soul touched my arm and said,
"You're already wonderful."
If a person standing next to me
had said that, I might have deflected
the truth of it, but this woman,
so ancient and good, who rivets
with a look and woos with a lovely
jangle of voice—there's no dismissing her.
So I stopped everything to gaze full upon
"You're already wonderful,"
lit up and sizzling in my mind,
and I thanked holy love
for her doggedness and charm.

Here in the Room 🍵

What have you done to keep the stories of your family and of your own life?

Imagine that the Holy Spirit arrives as a wise woman and sits with you here in the Room. She's come to help you remember aspects of your spiritual journey that you've forgotten. Spend some time talking with her. Perhaps she will encourage you to draw symbols or write down phrases that represent important moments in your story.

For the next few days, try to be more aware of the various expressions you make—the sighs and moans, the laughter, exclamations, and tears. Try to trace those expressions back to their roots—your emotions, worries, pain, enjoyment, and so forth. Invite the wise woman/Holy Spirit to accompany you as you examine your experience and what it means.

Ask the wise woman to accompany you this week as you dream and to help you remember your dreams and consider what they mean.

Ask the wise woman to help you envision the future God wants you to help create.

CHAPTER 24

Is prayer a request or a response?

My soul is satisfied as with a rich feast,
and my mouth praises you with joyful lips
when I think of you on my bed,
and meditate on you in the watches of
the night;
for you have been my help,
and in the shadow of your wings I sing
for joy.
My soul clings to you;
your right hand upholds me.

Psalm 63:5–8

From time to time, I still find myself in situations where people pray spontaneously and out loud, and I get annoyed when someone yammers on at God as though talking with a good buddy who wants to hear their detailed gripes and wants. But if you look at the book of Psalms, you'll find some similarities between Bible prayer and annoying prayer. Sometimes the psalmist is really full of himself. Often he wants God to blast his enemies straight to hell in the most painful and humiliating way possible. It's tempting to skim past those psalms, feeling rather embarrassed for God who must bear the responsibility for Scripture that has, after all, been divinely inspired.

What a foolhardy thing for God to do—give us access to divine life through what is best described as conversation. As a fiction writer, I study ordinary conversation all the time, and—I must be frank—human beings are rarely at their best when talking. We're so sloppy and repetitive and unclear and overbearing. Most of us have yet to learn the most critical requisite of good conversation: the ability to be quiet and listen. Even in civilized meetings, our egos and agendas get in the way, complicating processes and upsetting the people with whom we're supposed to be working. Little wonder that we make such a mess of prayer.

But God has never been afraid of messes. If you doubt that, just dip into the Bible and take note of the people God has used to accomplish holy deeds. It appears that God will use just about anybody—shepherd boys, prostitutes, old men with blood on their hands, and young girls having no apparent credentials for major theological enterprise. In fact, let's consider an important player in God's big scheme, Mary of Nazareth. One of the most famous divine conversations in all history happened between this girl and the angel Gabriel.

In the sixth month the angel Gabriel was sent by God to a town in Galilee called Nazareth, to a virgin engaged to a man whose name was Joseph, of the house of David. The virgin's name was Mary. And he came to her and said, "Greetings, favored one! The Lord is with you." But she was much perplexed by his words and pondered what sort of greeting this might be. The angel said to her, "Do not be afraid, Mary, for you have found favor with God. And now, you will conceive in your womb and bear a son, and you will name him Jesus. He will be great, and will be called the Son of the Most High, and the Lord God will give to him the throne of his ancestor David. He will reign over the house of Jacob forever, and of his kingdom there will be no end." Mary said to the angel, "How can this be, since I am a virgin?" The angel said to her, "The Holy Spirit will come upon you, and the power of the Most High will overshadow you; therefore the child to be born will be holy; he will be called Son of God. And now, your relative Elizabeth in her old age has also conceived a son; and this is the sixth month for her who was said to be barren. For nothing will be impossible with God." Then Mary said, "Here am I, the servant of the Lord; let it be with me according to your word." Then the angel departed from her.

—Luke 1:26–38

I think the Lord chose a young girl for this mission because a girl in the fervor of adolescence is able to harbor dreams and goals that border on the absurd. A girl just coming into her womanhood is open enough and feisty enough to stand there and talk to an angel, even question the information ("So, how will this happen if I've never had sex??"). And a young woman who is convinced that divine love has called upon her help— well, she just can't be stopped. She's stubborn and resilient and more optimistic than people who have become sensible and set in their ways. Mary's story is a reminder of how miraculous the teenage years can be. We become distracted by the mood swings and silences and fits of rebellion and questionable friends, but we forget how a girl's soul can open up and how willing she can become when she understands that God is truly interested in her life, her choices, and her future.

Mary's conversation with Gabriel—and by proxy, with God—is a wonderful example of what prayer truly is: our response to God's voice. This wasn't simply a matter of Gabriel telling Mary what would happen. By including Mary's detailed response, the Gospel writer implies that she had a choice. It was her body, after all. She was the one who must figure out a way to tell Joseph and her parents what was happening, and who would have to wait in faith while Joseph planned to break their engagement, before the angel spoke to him too. Mary was the one who felt the growth of a child within her while deflecting the glances of those in the community who concluded it was a bastard. She would give birth far from her mother and the midwife, surrounded by farm animals. She and Joseph and the child would live as refugees in another country. They would watch their son grow into his manhood and feel his way toward a destiny neither of them understood. The end of all this? Watching her child die by torture and in complete public humiliation.

Mary may have never conversed with Gabriel again, but there's no doubt that her life was one long prayer, a continuous response to the unfolding of God's action. The Gospel of Luke says that she prayed through pondering, holding things deep in her heart.[9] Sometimes I'm sure her conversation with the Divine included tears and waiting. When all we do is sit in the Room, quiet and weary, waiting and wondering, we are praying in a way that moves far beyond our words and reason.

Silent prayer can be unnerving; it takes practice to be truly quiet with God because we're so used to putting everything into words. We know how to complain and request. But in the silence we have no idea what might emerge. When we listen without knowing what to expect, we are forced into a new realm of openness. To be silent and waiting in the Room with God can feel as vulnerable as being naked in front of our doctor. Who knows what the examination will reveal? And how can we fight a diagnosis we've not yet heard? There's nothing to do but wait and no stance to take except to trust in God's love.

This depiction of a prayer life is quite different from the stories held up to me back when I was trying to be effective at prayer. If I were an effective pray-er, then I would present my requests in such a way that God would answer them. The real "prayer warriors" (a real term used in some circles) were those people who had documented all their asked and answered prayers—with dates and details. In other words, if your prayer moved God to action, then you were good at prayer.

Actually, each one of us could keep a list of all the ways in which God's love touches us. But must we consider the correspondence between our needs and God's works to be our personal track record of prayer? This seems far removed from a young girl hearing from God, asking honest questions, and then responding with love and trust.

When we respond to divine love, the experience of prayer will change us. It changed Mary—from a girl just going about her life to a woman who birthed divinity into our existence. Why should we think that God has no miracles to birth through each one of us?

The thing about God's voice is that,
even when it's booming and determined,
the point of its origin is inside me
somewhere, almost like a little seed
in my belly, sprouting desires and dreams
and courage—you really have no idea
the magnitude of these ideas,
the impossibility, the freaked-out nature
of my holy meditations.
If people knew what goes on in my belly
sometimes, when God Almighty is growing
and chuckling and, frankly,
straining my nerves—if people knew
the kinds of things that wake me up at
night, well, they would put me
on hormones or something, maybe

*painkillers or, perhaps, they would
just make certain I never got to
speak before large audiences.*

Here in the Room ☕️

Over the next several days, practice listening. Listen to everything—traffic sounds, nature sounds, speaking sounds, and the sounds of peace and quiet. Try to listen with great attention for five or ten minutes every day. Do this during a coffee/tea break, if that helps.

Then, gradually tune in to God's voice. This voice will come through many of the sounds you have already been noticing. It will also emerge as you partake of the arts—books, music, paintings, dance, and so forth. You will hear God's voice during worship or while your children are playing.

Try to spend a few moments each day quietly listening for God. Don't say anything or ask for anything. Or if you do ask for something, may it be, "God, help me tune in to your voice."

CHAPTER 25

What does it mean to pray with others?

Praise the LORD!
I will give thanks to the LORD with
    my whole heart,
    in the company of the upright,
        in the congregation.
Great are the works of the LORD,
    studied by all who delight in them.

Psalm 111:1–2

A group of Christians I worked with years ago had regular meetings to discuss the plans and needs of our organization and the community it served. Often we would grow passionate in our recitations of who needed our prayers—but we wouldn't actually pray there and then. We would continue through the meeting's agenda, and by then everyone was ready to eat. But one time, after we had adjourned, I noticed an older married couple sitting together quietly, not moving toward the meal. I came up to them and realized that they were praying for the needs we had mentioned. This didn't surprise me; of all the people in that organization, these two demonstrated most consistently the character of Jesus. For them, prayer was a normal part of their married partnership. And on the occasions when I prayed with them, I could feel the difference—in the atmosphere and in myself.

Conversation with God is not always a solitary affair, just as many of our other conversations involve more than one person. As Christians we have a built-in family, a fellowship of believers, and one of our chief tasks as the family of God is to maintain a running conversation about the things that are important to us.

Communal prayer strengthens the bond among Christians. When we pray with our brothers and sisters in Christ, we are sharing the interior self. When we open up and make known our personal needs and ask others to pray for them, we are revealing ourselves to our faith community. Although sometimes this vulnerability results in injury—when a member of that community uses knowledge wrongly, for example, or takes it outside the family—most of the time such prayer brings us closer together. As we learn more about one another's needs and struggles, we can develop empathy and grow more sensitive to others' situations.

Praying with others can also allow the Holy Spirit to confirm a message or direction. When people pray as a group, and more than one person in that group feels the weight of a particular need or situation, this can be a clear sign that God is revealing the need or situation so that the group can attend to it.

When Christians gather together, all listening for God's voice, God's voice might become translated through the voices of several people present. It was in such a group setting that the Holy Spirit told the Christians of the Antioch church to set apart Saul and Barnabas for specific ministry.[10] Unfortunately, many of us in today's church are not very open to that sort of leading by the Holy Spirit—our Pentecostal brothers and sisters could offer some experience in that regard. Still, people who pray together can grow in their sensitivity to the Spirit's guidance.

Praying in community can strengthen and encourage those present. I have participated in small prayer groups in which, on a certain evening, we would all end up in tears over a particular situation we were praying about. Maybe it was some horrible problem one person was enduring, and the rest of us mourned with her as we prayed. I have also witnessed one person giving a specific Bible verse or prayer or poem to another person in the group, words for that person to hold onto in the coming week. Together, we can pool our resources, our memories of God's presence, and our knowledge of the Scriptures.

There is always some danger in group settings, just as there is danger when a person sets out on a spiritual journey alone. If group prayer is not facilitated well, it can become a gripe session, or people might reveal more than is healthy for them or the group. Group prayer should not be confused with group therapy or used as such. If individuals choose not to act or speak with kindness and integrity, disaster can result—one person confronting another about his or her sin, someone gossiping about people outside the group in the guise of sharing prayer requests, or one person pushing an agenda or making speeches. If you are involved with a group that has become unhealthy, deal with that issue head-on—and if no change is forthcoming, get out.

Some people have prayer partners, one other individual with whom they meet and pray regularly. Prayer partnerships can lend wonderful support to the spiritual life, and another bonus is a good friendship. Because praying together involves intimacy, it's best to avoid a relationship in which sexual attraction could develop. By the same token, many couples in committed relationships have enriched their lives by praying together regularly.

As you develop your friendship with God, you will also develop a relationship with God's many other friends. Through prayer you will commune with brothers and sisters in the faith. You can also commune with those of faith who have passed on, the loved ones and other saints you can include in your praying.

My name—some syllables
attached to me since birth,
ordinary yet intensely special.
My name—used all the time
by people who love me
and by some who don't.
My name—uttered one evening
by a person who believes
that God is love
and that God loves me.
My name—coming from that voice,

suddenly rang with presence.
Another person spoke the syllables
of my name with such bravery and
tenderness. Such love—willing
to approach Divine Everything
on my behalf. The sound of that person
praying my name—it continues forever
in my mysterious life,
through years and doubts and silence.

Here in the Room

Who, if anyone, do you really love listening to when she or he prays? Why do you think you respond in this way?

Use these images to help you think about prayer in community:
- » family around the dinner table
- » members of a softball team
- » doctors and nurses tending to a patient
- » explorers scaling a mountainside

Add some images of your own, and roll them around inside your imagination.

Spend time in the next couple of weeks thinking about two or three people you know who might be willing to pray in a group with you. Make a list of several different methods for praying together. For instance, you could pray the rosary or the Psalms, use the Book of Common Prayer or other liturgical resources. You could find someone to guide you in learning to sit together in silent, contemplative prayer. You could sing as part of your praying, or take turns writing prayers. Group prayer does not require everyone to be spontaneous or to pray aloud.

PART SIX

Attention

Eternity is with us, inviting our contemplation perpetually, but we are too frightened, lazy, and suspicious to respond: too arrogant to still our thought, and let divine sensation have its way. It needs industry and goodwill if we would make that transition: for the process involves a veritable spring-cleaning of the soul, a turning-out and rearrangement of our mental furniture, a wide opening of closed windows, that the notes of the wild birds beyond our garden may come to us fully charged with wonder and freshness, and drown with their music the noise . . . within. Those who do this, discover that they have lived in a stuffy world, while their inheritance was a world of morning-glory; where every tit-mouse is a celestial messenger, and every thrusting bud is charged with the full significance of life.

Evelyn Underhill, *Practical Mysticism*[11]

After seventeen years of marriage, I have developed a detailed awareness of my husband. I have countless "Jim" files in my mind and heart. I know what he likes and doesn't like, how he is affected by lack of sleep or a new challenge. I know how to approach him when he's having a bad day.

This awareness hasn't just happened on its own. A continuing challenge of marriage is to discipline myself to pay attention to a person who is around me so much that I mistakenly think I can understand and love him without exerting much effort. Proximity and habit aren't enough to nourish a marriage. Some people live together for decades without learning to pay attention, and so one day they realize that while they have moved through days and years of activity and habit, something that should have been tended carefully has deteriorated.

Paying attention is a spiritual discipline. Without it, most aspects of life will sooner or later fall into serious disrepair. It's not enough to simply get through the day—not if we have any aspirations for an abundant life, a life of friendship with God.

CHAPTER 26

How do you truly wake up?

You cause the grass to grow for the cattle,
and plants for people to use,
to bring forth food from the earth,
and wine to gladden the human heart,
oil to make the face shine,
and bread to strengthen the human heart.

Psalm 104:14–15

Caribou Coffee is my favorite supplier of late-afternoon cappuccinos. The company motto, printed on cups and other items, is *Life is short. Stay awake for it.* As a Christian, I believe that life is not short but eternal. However, if we're not awake for it, life feels not only short but extremely limited and desperate. When unawake, we live by the deadline and the necessity. We don't experience wonder and have no sense of divine love or guidance. All we know is our own noise and movement.

There's a comedy bit in which one person shouts, "Where are you?" and is startled when the other person, standing inches away, says softly, "Right here." This is an apt description of our God-awareness. We experience pain or come up against a problem and start shrieking for God to come help us—and God quietly taps us on the shoulder and reminds us that we don't need to yell.

Whenever we feel the need to call upon God, a good spiritual practice is to say to ourselves, "God is already here." We don't have to send a summons to a faraway deity and then wait for divine presence to show up. Before we know that we need God's help, God is already standing right beside us, waiting for us to notice.

We cultivate awareness of God in many ways. Here are just a few.

We notice God's presence in the created world. When we walk through a neighborhood and notice forty different types of flowers and trees, feel the breeze against our face, and smell rain on the way, we know that all of this didn't happen by itself. Even as we watch construction crews at work, we know that the wood, steel, and everything in between was found right here on this planet. Also, human beings have the ability of thought and coordination to invent things such as espresso machines. Thus, on just one street God's presence fairly shouts at us.

We experience God's presence through other people. Human beings can be irritating, rude, or dangerous, sometimes all on the same bus ride. But they also lend unexpected kindness or help, they usher in a moment of humor, they do something heroic, they offer encouragement and wisdom. God comes to us in strangers, neighbors, friends, and family members. God also comes to us in people we've never met but who help us through their art or their work—or save our life through a blood transfusion. Sometimes we look into the eyes of another person and are startled by the wisdom and power that we see, or by the tenderness and care that shines out of that person. All of these are glimmers of divine love evident through human experience and human nature.

We are aware of God through sacred story and ritual. As Christians we recognize the Bible as sacred text. Within its stories, genealogies, historical chronicles, poems, proverbs, and letters, God has given us important understanding about eternal reality. Jesus tells a little story about seeds or sheep, a wedding or a crafty employee, and we know that divine love has offered us a revelatory gift. Jesus decides to depict God as a father who takes back a rebellious child, and we perceive a crucial message: "See, God loves you that much and more. God is always waiting for you to come home, is always waiting to hug you."

The liturgies, prayers, and rituals that Christians and Jews have practiced for thousands of years have survived, at least in part, because they became windows into the mystery of our union with God and one another. The very fact that people have poured their faith and love into the movements and phrases has livened and imbued them with holy power from one generation to the next.

We are aware of God through God's voice within our own soul. Even though I'm a word person, I'm glad that Western culture has begun to swing more toward visual information such as movies. We need to connect to the part of us that is not so rational, word-oriented, logical, and scientific. For centuries we silenced the more mysterious parts of the human soul because we thought scientific inquiry and rational thinking precluded dreams, visions, and intuition. We are beginning to believe in visions again and have begun to accept that dreams have something to tell us. Even in the business world, leaders are encouraging us to follow our hunches and be more open to meditation, group retreats, and other practices that used to be relegated to spiritual discussions. We are learning to be whole souls again.

After thousands of prayers and moments of silence in God's presence, the soul learns to sense what we cannot understand with reason, theology, or psychology. If we enter the Room often enough and stay long enough to sense the Holy, then we will learn to perceive what the Holy Spirit communicates to us. The more we allow this intuitive part of our faith to grow, the more confident we will become in our ability to sense God's heart.

My heartbeat has always quickened
in the presence of a particular shade
of blue-green; I don't know why,
except it reminds me of color-by-number
books and childhood afternoons
when I would create, one defined piece
after another, an ocean or shadowed valley.
I had never seen an ocean,
but that blue-green on a page
where a bright dream appeared in stages—

Here in the Room

Do something today (or this week) that fills you with wonder. Don't ask yourself if it's a spiritual activity. Don't go automatically to a religious place—your assignment is to ask yourself what takes your breath away, and then find that experience, or something close to it.

Maybe you get jazzed by the arts—galleries or concerts or theater-in-the-park. Your heart might swell to its capacity when you get together with close friends for a little party or a road trip. Or, the act that feeds your soul may be private: reading a favorite poet or novelist or spending four hours walking along a river. Whatever your "wonder" is, go find it and spend time with it. Ask God to wake you up.

Then, after you've found your wonder, make some "wonder appointments" for the coming weeks. Get away from the television and e-mail, from housework and committee meetings. Do you really think that God of the universe means for you to live, one day to the next, groggy and numb?

If you want to be a little daring . . .

Go looking for a lively woman who can teach you how to wake up. It may be an aunt, a neighbor, a local artist or teacher you admire, or some elderly woman who has been entertaining you for years by showing up at church with a different hat every month. Most of us know someone who inspires in us the desire to become the best version of ourselves. Ask that someone over for tea or out for an afternoon. Waking up is a skill, and somewhere close by is a wide-awake person who can help you learn.

CHAPTER 27

How do spiritual traditions aid attentiveness?

Your word is a lamp to my feet
and a light to my path. . . .
Your decrees are wonderful;
therefore my soul keeps them.
The unfolding of your words gives light;
it imparts understanding to the simple.

Psalm 119: 105, 129–130

Sometimes it's not enough to cultivate awareness of God all around us. Sometimes spiritual life needs focus and direction, or it needs to delve into mysteries that lie beyond our perception or wisdom. We may bring our whole self to attentiveness, may bring an open heart and the desire for friendship, but God did not design us to be self-sufficient and to enjoy divine love

204

only in our own way in a private space. Even the early Christian mystics, living out in deserts and mountains for years on end, learned that some kind of community was necessary for balanced spiritual growth. There will always be a gap where our ability ends and eternal mystery begins. This gap is bridged, at least in part, by traditional practices of the faith such as sacraments, liturgy, and pilgrimage. These practices are the church's way of experiencing holy life with focused attention.

Sacrament merges eternal mysteries with physical matter. We eat what appears to be ordinary bread and wine, but we believe that in doing so we take into ourselves the body and blood of Jesus. Baptisms, weddings, taking vows for ordained or religious life, and anointing with oil the sick and dying—these focus our attention on specific aspects of our connection with God.

Liturgy provides words, phrases, rhythm, movement, silence, music, and prayer. Through all of these we involve the physical senses as well as thought and emotion. So even if I'm not feeling connected to God this morning, as I move through liturgy I act as if I were connected. I act out my friendship with the help of some very effective props, and often as my body worships, my emotions follow.

Pilgrimage brings spiritual attentiveness to a whole new level, because we strip away everything except movement toward a specific location. We commit to that particular journey with its particular history. Often, liturgy and sacrament are part of pilgrimage, giving the experience triple potency.

Traditional practices of Christianity are like the ruts in ancient Roman roads. They have been traveled for so many centuries by so many people that all we have to do is step into them. We don't even have to know the way, because the road knows it for us. We can simply follow that path so worn that it is shiny smooth and deeper than the surfaces around it.

We're not the least bit ashamed to follow a recipe for carrot cake that originated with Great-Great-Grandma. In fact, we're proud to have something so authentic and good, a recipe that has gathered layers of love as it passed through the generations. The fact that so many women before us have served this particular carrot cake on special occasions makes us treasure it all the more.

Yet when it comes to spirituality, many of us feel that the time-tested practice is of little use to us—either it is so familiar that we ignore it, or so foreign that we avoid it. But why must we reinvent everything? Why start from scratch—whether making a cake or making friends—when there are people who can hand us a recipe or make an introduction?

Our friendship with God acquires new dimensions when we attend to it through the enduring practices of Christian community.

The first prayer I learned was
"Now I Lay Me Down to Sleep."
Later came the Our Father.
There were the favorite songs, such as
"Amazing Grace" and "O Sacred Head."
Even later, the prayers of the Eucharist.
So many days I walk to the rhythm
"Lamb of God, who takes away the sins of
the world"—that runs its continuous course
in my heart, reverberating through the
hours. In speaking the old words
I sound a note, which sets off grand
harmonics, sympathetic tones in the
halls of heaven. I whisper,
"the Lord my soul to keep"
and create in that very spot a refuge,
before I can even lay me down.

Here in the Room ☕———————

Find a written form of Christian liturgy—in the Book of
Common Prayer, in a church missal, or from the Internet. If you
had never heard them before, what words and phrases would
stand out? Choose a phrase or a sentence and write it on a blank
piece of paper. Read the words aloud, listening to their sound.
Play around with them, inventing a poem or song, adding colors
and designs. Let the liturgy work on you in a new way.

Create a pilgrimage for yourself. Choose a location or a series of
locations meaningful to you, and design a trip that will help you
focus upon the meaning. One woman journeyed to her home-
town with a collection of beautiful stones and placed one at each
significant location of her childhood: the site of the house she
lived in, the school she attended, and so on. This was her way of
making peace with her past. You can create the kind of pilgrimage that fits your needs and situation.

Think of at least one older woman whom you consider a true
friend of God. What do you know about her spiritual practice?
If you feel so inclined, ask her about it.

CHAPTER 28

What is significant about God as parent?

As a father has compassion for his children,
so the LORD has compassion for those who
fear him.

Psalm 103:13

I have calmed and quieted my soul,
like a weaned child with its mother.

Psalm 131:2

E ach one of us has a built-in means of paying attention to God: the parent-child relationship. This applies regardless of what that relationship has been like. It even applies if we have not experienced much in the way of being someone's child or parent.

Let's imagine that your child just spent her first semester away at college, and she's coming home for nearly three weeks of holiday break. You have been planning, at least mentally, all the things you want to do with her and the conversations you hope to have. But—we know where this is going—the moment she lands at home, she's on the phone and headed out the door to connect with her friends. Already most of her time is spoken for, and it doesn't include hanging out with Mom. And when you do manage to grab her for a trip to the mall or for lunch, the flow of conversation isn't at all what you had imagined. The intimacy that's so important to you is on the periphery for her.

There are natural, healthy reasons that young adult children don't linger with the folks at home when they return from their journeys. Still, the disappointment we feel when our own babies can't sit with us awhile must be somewhat representative of how our lives frustrate divine love. As parents, we know that our children really do need a sustained connection to us—for our wisdom, our understanding, our experience, and our company. We believe that they will do much better in life if we are allowed to continue our loving interaction with them. We don't want to run their lives or make them overly dependent on us, but we fear for their welfare when they cut us off and stay away.

It's not overreaching to put God in this parental role. Hear what God says through the prophet Hosea:

> *When Israel was a child, I loved him,*
> *   and out of Egypt I called my son.*
> *The more I called them,*
> *   the more they went from me;*
> *they kept sacrificing to the Baals,*
> *   and offering incense to idols.*

Yet it was I who taught Ephraim to walk,
*   I took them up in my arms;*
*   but they did not know that I healed them.*
I led them with cords of human kindness,
*   with bands of love*
I was to them like those
*   who lift infants to their cheeks.*
I bent down to them and fed them.

                —Hosea 11:1–4

There's always risk in giving God human attributes because they are tainted by human experience. But Jesus unapologetically called God the equivalent of "Dad" or "Papa." Jesus could do this because he was fully human and knew firsthand the qualities of relationship between parent and child. Jesus could also use such language for God because he was fully divine and understood more clearly than any other human being the depth of God's love toward human beings.

I suspect that, in his divine capacity, Jesus knew that *father* was an inadequate representation for what he was trying to communicate. He undoubtedly chose that image for the Divine because in Jewish culture the father was the ultimate protector and provider for the family. The Jewish ideal father was both gentle and just, patiently taught his children to live well, and helped them find their place in the world. Jesus was able to choose the father image for God because Joseph had given him such a loving experience of father-son relationship—we really underappreciate Joseph's role in bringing God closer to our understanding!

Whatever Jesus' reasons for calling God our Father, we can't dismiss what he was getting at: the energy and attention God directs our way is at the very least as nurturing, as tender and intentional, as the love we lavish upon our own children. We know it's not enough simply to take care of our babies; we must spend time just being with them. As they grow up and develop lives of their own, we desperately hope they will continue to desire time just being with us. Sometimes we drive ourselves to utter foolishness trying to demonstrate to our kids how welcome they are and that we want them around, just to sit and talk and laugh and enjoy simple things with us. (I mean, really, why else would we keep doing their laundry?)

Each of us has experienced, in a unique way, being someone's child. From our experiences we know how parental love helped us, and we also know how the failure of parental love wounded us. Many of us also understand parent-child love from our position as parents or stepparents, and we can bring these experiences into the Room as well. By exploring what it means to be parented, and what it means to parent, we have yet another way of exploring who God-as-parent is to us.

It took years to realize that I avoided
seeing You as mother because I was afraid
of how tender that experience might be.
If, in its relentless and fierce affection,
the cosmos could become so warm and
pliable, then the harsh and brittle
parts of me would surely cave in.

*To be cuddled is to weep sloppily
and know weakness, to give in
and abandon anger, to be held aloft
and hear whispers so intimate
my heart might be transformed.*

Here in the Room 🍵_____

Bring into the Room your happy memories of being someone's child. Think of times when your mother or father paid good attention to you, really listened to you. Think of times when a parent grieved to see you sad or ill or in trouble. Remember affection, a sense of humor, or the way a parent taught you to do something new.

As you drift through those memories, consider that God of the universe was present in the love of mother or father. Imagine that those good memories were not merely of the people in your life but of God's involvement with you.

What do you do with bad memories? Imagine them differently, as if that mother or father said and did the loving thing after all. Having been hurt by a parent, you understand very well what would have been the loving thing for him or her to do. God has given you this ability to know what should have happened, how you should have been helped or instructed or protected. The fact that you can know how your mother or father should have treated you is an indication that there was always that possibility of being loved, and that this is how God loves you through past, present, and future.

If there are children in your life, pay close attention to how you care for them, how your heart desires their good and wants their company. Notice how glorious it feels to give that child a hug or make her laugh or explain something that will help her cope with life. With every loving act you carry out, remind yourself that this love and wonder that you experience, being able to love the child, is a mere hint of God's response to you. In other words, allow your experience of being a parent to inform your awareness of God's presence with you.

I encourage you to shift your mental and emotional sense of God as parent—if you have thought of God as father, then spend some time contemplating God as mother. This might be more difficult than you expect. Think of how differently you relate to your biological father from how you relate to your mother. Think of how your expectations of one are different from your expectations of the other. For instance, the first thing that may happen when you see your mother is that the two of you hug. Or perhaps you tend to talk to your father more about your accomplishments than about how you feel. These differences in your approach to a father or mother figure have real consequences in how you pray and in how you imagine God responding to you.

CHAPTER 29

What brings you desolation?

> *My God, my God, why have you forsaken me?*
> *Why are you so far from helping me, from*
>   *the words of my groaning?*
> *O my God, I cry by day, but you do not*
>   *answer;*
>   *and by night, but find no rest.*
>
>   *Psalm 22:1–2*

Desolation sounds rather old-fashioned. It's a biblical word that carries a sense of heaviness. Though we tend not to use it in everyday conversation, sometimes it comes up when the topic is a national disaster or a pervasive social problem.

But language can get in the way. You and I are well acquainted with desolation, as St. Ignatius of Loyola used the term:

obtuseness of soul, turmoil within it, an impulsive motion toward low and earthly things, or disquiet from various agitations and temptations. These move one toward lack of faith and leave one without hope and without love. One is completely listless, tepid, and unhappy, and feels separated from our Creator and Lord.[12]

Ignatius considered desolation to be the work of an evil spirit inside a person, bringing doubt, darkness, temptation, and other unhelpful qualities. Whether or not you believe in the devil or in demons, you can—and really must—acquaint yourself with desolation, because it's a great indicator in your life. Think of desolation as located at the dark end of the spectrum that is your spiritual intuition. Desolation is what you sense when your soul is disturbed, troubled, or feeling an unhelpful weight that demands your attention. Desolation registers within you when something is not right.

Women have always been experts at detecting desolation. When men are ready to take action and solve problems, women grab their elbows and say, "I don't feel right about this." A famous example of desolation is when Pontius Pilate's wife warned him not to harm Jesus of Nazareth. She'd been warned in a dream, and she told her husband he'd better watch his step. Unfortunately, Pilate thought he knew more than she did about political and tactical matters, and his course could not be corrected by a wife's intuition. He was not the first man, nor would he be the last, to ignore such signals.

Unfortunately, even we women have been conditioned to live with desolation rather than heed its warning and change our lives. By the time we're in our teens and twenties, many of us think it's normal to be tired too much of the time, and to have a continuing sadness, and to carry with us unresolved conflicts, unspoken griefs, and unhealed wounds. God designed our souls to speak to us when all is not well, but if we decide that it is normal not to be well and that it's part of our job to simply learn to accommodate our desolation, then God's voice within us cannot bring the change that is so necessary.

What are the signs of desolation? A gnawing inside about a decision you are about to make or have already made. A whispering worry that won't subside. A feeling of sadness more substantial than the fleeting case of the blues we all get from time to time. Sometimes desolation is laced with dread or foreboding; sometimes it's the strong sense that something isn't right, or that you have within some difficult matter to attend to.

It's important to remember that dark emotions are not always signs of the spiritual intuition we know as desolation. Mindset, physiology, and natural rhythms can cause very similar feelings. For instance, if I enter a conversation on the defensive because I've heard that this person doesn't approve of the way I do my job, I will interpret everything she says through this filter. What she might say in humor I will interpret as sarcasm or ridicule, and my emotions will respond accordingly, even if they are falsely informed.

Emotions are influenced by fatigue, diet, illness, menstrual cycle, and the weather. Some of us are more naturally depressed during winter months or when it's raining. Some of us are more sensitive during certain times of our cycle or when we have a headache. Stress does all kinds of things to us emotionally. Sometimes our inner darkness is merely the sign of a natural phase of life—grief is the appropriate response to loss, and anxiety is the natural result of stressful events.

I offer two stories, one an example of emotions that did not spring from spiritual intuition, and the other an example of true desolation.

As a young adult I went through an orientation program of several weeks to prepare for a two-year teaching assignment overseas. I felt deeply called to this assignment, and the stimulating classes and programs only added to my anticipation of the work ahead. But about two weeks into the orientation I began waking up in horrible anxiety. I cried a lot, out of acute sadness, and endured a fairly constant feeling of panic. This went on for days. I feared that it was the Holy Spirit telling me not to go after all. Yet my desires and gifts fit this job so well, and every choice along the way had seemed the logical and right next step. I talked to one of the staff counselors, and after a while he concluded that this was a natural response to anticipating a drastic break from home and my family. I had never lived away from home on a long-term basis. Also, my father was quite ill from a degenerative and incurable disease, and part of my crying and panicking was a form of anticipatory grief at the prospect of his dying while I was away.

Once the counselor pinpointed these issues, it all made sense. Within a few days, the tears were gone and the anxiety had abated. These disturbing feelings were not God telling me to change my plans. Rather, they were natural responses to major shifts in my life. The years I spent in that assignment were rich and difficult and among the most rewarding of my life—I was exactly where I should have been. Thank goodness a wise counselor was available to prevent my coming to a different conclusion.

A few years later, a friend of mine began to experience pain, confusion, doubt, and dread as she contemplated going through with a marriage. She was in her forties and had never married. Her fiancé, most of us thought, was a very good catch. My friend could cite many reasons this was a good decision. They shared common interests, abilities, and experiences; they both were ready to quit the single life; she got along well with his family, and so on. But the awful feeling in the pit of her stomach would not go away. She ended up breaking the engagement, which left her feeling battered and brought painful criticism from some friends who doubtless thought this might be her last chance at married life. But she had attended to those signs of desolation, and she knew she had done the right thing. (She married a couple of years later, to a man she hit it off with immediately— no desolation there!)

We have all experienced desolation, even if we might not have called it that. We endure it for days, or weeks, or much longer before ending a relationship that isn't good for us. We finally listen to it when we decide to resign from a job for which we are ill suited. Because such disturbing deep-down feelings persist, we learn at last to change a habit of self-condemnation. Some desolation is the direct result of sin; we have done wrong, have caused damage, have turned away from God, and the darkness within us attests to that and motivates us to make a change. We ask someone's forgiveness.

This kind of discernment takes practice. It requires an inner quietness that allows us to listen closely to what our soul is telling us. Sometimes discernment requires a spiritual director or counselor who can help us sort through all the shadows and sensations.

Contrary to what I used to believe,
it doesn't help that much to name the
darkness. Something named does not
necessarily change.
What if I must touch the dark thing,
talk with it, walk alongside it,
allow its speech to move me?
Can I let it wash over me,
can I embrace it for a closer look?
Lord, you come in bright praise,
in wisdom that shines,
but then those times when your brilliance
is rumbling and thick with shadows,
an ache reverberating,
a lesson yet unlearned.

Here in the Room ☕️

> » Recall a time when dark emotions filled you because of mindset.
>
> » Recall a time when dark emotions filled you because of body chemistry or cycle.
>
> » Recall a time when dark emotions filled you because of natural life seasons and events.

Now remember a time when you experienced deep wisdom, only it was in the form of desolation. How did you know that this dark emotion had real meaning for you? How did you respond?

What have you learned through the years about interpreting your deep feelings, even the unpleasant ones?

Come up with two or three guiding principles that will help you pay attention to interior desolation.

CHAPTER 30

What brings you consolation?

The LORD is my shepherd, I shall not want.
He makes me lie down in green pastures;
he leads me beside still waters;
he restores my soul.

. . .

Even though I walk through the darkest valley,
I fear no evil;
for you are with me.

Psalm 23:1–4

Nearly twenty years ago, my mother left my father in the hospital and made the hour-long drive home. She had done this many times, because his advanced diabetes had landed him in intensive care repeatedly as his various body systems began to stall or shut down altogether. But this night was different; Mom understood that Dad would never come home again. She reached home and entered the empty house and knew deep in her bones that he was dying. He had been close to death numerous times, but this really was the end. What darkness, and what loneliness, to know that so clearly.

She didn't expect to sleep at all that night—she often had trouble sleeping, with her husband miles away and suffering. She expected to have a "nervous spell," a form of anxiety attack that she had grappled with through the years. But that night she went to sleep quickly and slept soundly. Even more amazing, the next morning she awoke with the feeling that a great weight had lifted. It was unlike anything she had experienced during those long years of Dad's illness and the numerous frantic trips to the hospital.

I suppose you could argue that Mom experienced this peace because she had turned a difficult corner by accepting that her husband would die soon. But she had faced this prospect for a number of years, had expected him to die so many other times, had seen him in and out of comas, had stood at the bedside with other family members while the minister prayed and waited with them for death—and yet never before had she experienced this palpable sense of relief and weightlessness. Later she learned that, on that very night, without anyone knowing what had transpired at the hospital or what my mother was feeling, some people at her church had formed a prayer chain. They had literally prayed for her all through the night. And so she—and those of us close to her—accepted this deep consolation as a direct answer to prayer.

Consolation is exactly what it sounds like. Your soul is comforted, is relieved, is brightened, is filled with joy or hope or tranquility. Often, there's no real explanation for it—the Ignatian term for this is "consolation without cause." Sometimes consolation is not something that happens to you but something you finally recognize; it has been dwelling within you, helping your spirit respond to God's movement, and you've been too busy and worried and fearful to quiet yourself and notice it.

When Ignatius of Loyola spent long weeks recuperating from a serious battle injury, he passed the time reading. He asked for books on chivalry and romance, but the only books available were about Jesus and lives of the saints. Ignatius began to notice that he enjoyed imagining himself as the hero in a tale of chivalry, but after the daydream was over, he didn't feel content or happy at all. However, after imagining himself following the example of Jesus and the saints, he felt a deep peace and happiness. Perhaps because he was trapped in hours of solitude due to his injuries, he was forced to notice some of the deeper dynamics going on inside him. The consolation he experienced in his daydreams about saintly living eventually emerged so that he could recognize it and interpret it as an indication of what his life should become. That recognition formed his initial conversion to a faith-centered life.

This is how he described consolation:

> Under the word consolation I include every increase in hope, faith, and charity, and every interior joy which calls and attracts one toward heavenly things and to the salvation of one's soul, by bringing it tranquility and peace in its Creator and Lord.[13]

Consolation is your soul telling you what is helpful and what truly gives you joy. It is the Holy Spirit confirming to you that you are doing the right thing or that your spiritual perceptions are correct. Consolation is simply the result of your communion with God; it comes when, in the presence of divine love, your spirit chimes along harmoniously with the universe.

It's important not to confuse spiritual consolation with circumstances that simply make us feel good. In the same way we can experience difficult emotions due to circumstances or normal physical cycles, we can feel very light and happy thanks to a cold beer, a long-awaited rest, or some other temporary source of relief or enjoyment. Ignatius thought that when people were living in patterns of sin, the devil delivered to them false consolations so that they would not change their ways but remain in harmful patterns. This is similar to the unhelpful containers we looked at in chapter 2, the things we do in order to simply feel better rather than get better, the addictions that bring a relief of sorts, but a relief that is short-lived and no real solution. These things are not true consolations.

It's also important to understand that our spiritual resistance will sometimes prevent our recognizing or responding to consolation. Perhaps we feel, deep down, that we don't deserve to experience joy or relief. Or we have been taught to distrust our feelings and to give more validation to ideas that appear reasonable and correct. Sometimes we don't allow consolation to register because we avoid deep feelings of any kind. Profound emotion unnerves us, and so we don't give any more attention to it than we have to.

Another reason we don't always acknowledge consolation is that, like desolation, it requires some action on our part. Because consolation is designed to help us discern what is going on within us and around us, it's usually not enough just to recognize it. Discernment naturally leads us to say yes to an opportunity or to follow through with an action.

Consolation is yet another signal God gives us so that we can make good decisions and go in the direction our lives need to go. Both consolation and desolation train us to pay attention to our interior life and allow it to guide us. Sometimes consolation enables us to make hard choices because they are the right choices. One woman artist I know went back to work full-time because her husband needed to retire early. When she thought of all the creative time she would sacrifice, her feelings were not happy; nevertheless, as she pondered taking this step, consolation welled up within her and she made the change even though it would make her life more difficult in some ways. Sometimes the good choice we're making will have its shadow side, its negative effects, and so consolation dwells alongside some grief or pain or even anger.

One thing is clear: consolation is spiritual joy. The question is, are we ready to experience that sort of abundance? Are we willing to get lost in enjoyment, to cease trying to rein in our feelings and how we express them? Consolation that comes from God is powerful and life-changing. When we dare pay attention to that joy of our souls that is bigger than us and that cannot be tamed, well, we may find ourselves in the midst of conversion.

There was that time when everything
fell apart, and yes I cried
and yes people were not happy—
such a mess—but my steps did not falter
because it was the right thing to do.
I knew this not out of stubbornness but
by the way You pressed my heart
with light and warmth.
And I could never be a Stoic when
it comes to pain, but I could be a pilgrim
when it comes to bad weather,
just slog through mud and inconvenience,
already feeling the high-above sunlight,
and standing before an ancient altar
in a bright chapel miles from here.

Here in the Room

When have you sensed joy or peacefulness or comfort? In retrospect, could any of those experiences have come from God?

Each of us learns a particular set of interior signals that point out the right thing to do or the right way to go. What are those signals for you? How would you recognize when consolation is present within you?

Describe a time when you experienced false consolation—good feelings that did not inform or help you spiritually, that might have even distracted you from what you needed to be doing.

Women are often conditioned to distrust our feelings and to put little stock in our deeper movements of soul, whether consolation or desolation. What has your experience been in this area?

Now consider older generations of women in your family: your mother, aunts, and grandmothers. As nearly as you can recall, to what extent did they learn to trust their sense of consolation or desolation? How free were they to express when something was not right? And how well were they able to truly experience and express God's joy?

Invite those women to be with you now as you dwell here in the Room. Imagine them talking about what they know of consolation and desolation. Write down some of what they say.

Now, turn to all of them as a group, and ask, "Is it all right for me to experience God's joy?"

PART SEVEN

Engagement

Women generally profit more from reflecting on areas of giftedness, graces, breakthroughs and successes, recognizing how God has brought fruit into all dimensions of life. Women often need time to acknowledge their gifts and to take responsibility for their own lives, since they may not habitually do so. They may need to get in touch with their own initiative and responsibility in response to an initiating, enlivening and loving God.

KATHERINE DYCKMAN, MARY GARVIN,
AND ELIZABETH LIEBERT,
THE SPIRITUAL EXERCISES RECLAIMED[14]

Engagement has to do with action. Any mother knows there's a big difference between sending the kids outside to play and going out there to play with them. Engagement requires thought and effort; it costs time and energy. If any relationship is going to grow, then both parties must learn to engage.

One challenge of engaging in friendship with God is understanding what such engagement looks like. Of course it involves conversation—prayer. Most of us understand worship as engagement with God. But what else? Even as I write this material, I feel a little panic rising: Do I do enough in this relationship?

Actually, our days are full of opportunities to share actively in God's life. It helps if we look at some of these opportunities in more detail.

- CHAPTER 31 -

Why are your gifts important?

I praise you, for I am fearfully and wonderfully made.
Wonderful are your works;
that I know very well.
My frame was not hidden from you,
when I was being made in secret,
intricately woven in the depths of the earth.
Your eyes beheld my unformed substance.

Psalm 139:14–16

Much of what I offer to participants at writers' workshops is permission—and relief. I give them permission to simply do what they want to do: write poetry, compose a family history, work on that novel, or finally submit an article to a magazine or newspaper. Because we live in a celebrity culture that dismisses any creative work that hasn't made us rich and famous, most of us need permission to try—even in private—to write or paint. I offer relief to people by opening the valve to their desires. Many of them have already begun this process, or they wouldn't have come to a workshop to begin with. But it can be quite a release for another person to tell them that their desires matter and that they should act on them.

Once again we must consider our perceptions of God. Is God a rigid judge who makes everything a puzzle to be figured out, who makes us guess and strive for years before we know what we should do? Does God consider what we really like to do and then require us to take up the opposite of that as our career—because surely our dreams and desires are faulty—and, anyway, we need to build a little character and also save the world?

Do we believe that God is good, and that God loves us? Do we believe Jesus when he says that a good father won't give his children a stone when they ask for bread? These are desperately critical questions. If we don't believe that God is on our side, then every aspect of life becomes an engagement of the worst kind, a battle against a deity who is always out to thwart our movement, or a battle against our true self with its many gifts and desires.

This topic of giftedness is deep and wide, and I've explored it more specifically in a previous book, *The Soul Tells a Story: Engaging Creativity with Spirituality in the Writing Life.*[15] The main points to consider, for our purposes, are these:

Our own deep loves and desires point the way to our best gifts. Recently I met a man who gives seminars about zombie movies. He has loved zombie movies from the time he was a kid, and as an adult he now relates zombie movies to spiritual topics that interest young people. He is one of various people I've encountered who have turned a passion into work that benefits others.

What did you really enjoy doing as a child, before the adult world encroached upon your sensibilities? Are you doing now, in any form, what you used to enjoy doing so much back then? And if not, why not?

The boy Jesus didn't suddenly develop an interest in the Scriptures when he landed at the temple that day; a twelve-year-old will involve himself in what he already has an affinity for. I believe Jesus had especially loved the sacred texts of Judaism from an early age, and that love led him to the temple event and on into his life as teacher and prophet.

It's possible that for much of your life people and institutions have told you what you *should* enjoy. Perhaps you were physically oriented, loving sports of all kinds since you could hold a ball in your hands—and you were born into a family more interested in academics, the arts, or religious activities. Or you're an artist at heart but have made your living in the business world. Even so, you can pay attention to what you really enjoy, the topics and activities that make you happy. You may not be able to make a living or a career from a favorite hobby, but it doesn't hurt to explore the possibilities. And sometimes we use our best gifts outside of work hours.

Engaging with gifts involves dealing with negative pressure. Many of us who grew up in church developed strong ideas about what kind of careers and activities God approved of. If you were a Catholic boy who showed much promise at all when it came to religious action, academic ability, or spiritual passion—of course God must be calling you to be a priest! If you were a girl with those same qualities, then the convent was in your future. I grew up in an evangelical Protestant environment in which keen interest and ability concerning things religious or spiritual would elicit all sorts of predictions about your future as a missionary, preacher, or (if you were female) preacher's wife. Holy work and holy life were so narrowly defined that many good-hearted, well-intentioned people journeyed through years of damage, working hard in careers to which God never called them. Or, if they went into jobs and careers better suited to their gifts, they never quite shook the feeling that their lives were second-best to the lives they should have had, if they had done the holy thing.

The culture we live in values some gifts more than others. As a teenager and college student, I was quite involved with music. While it was satisfying to receive good response to my singing and composing, it was scary to realize how often people assumed I had achieved a certain level of spiritual maturity, only because I could articulate faith so well. Clearly some esteem was attached to my gifts simply because they were visible and vocal. I don't know that people expressed so much appreciation for the people who kept a balanced budget for our congregation, or the ones who were especially helpful with toddlers or with prayer. Even in our faith communities the culture of celebrity skews any healthy view of giftedness.

Sometimes the negative pressure against your giftedness is internal. You're a working mother with little time for hobbies, and your job is all right but not situated within your giftedness.

You discover a deep desire within you to study physics, or psychology, or architecture. You may have full support from your family, but *you* wonder if you're crazy, going to night classes and piling on more responsibility, not being at home so much.

Another negative pressure is popular culture's view of women and their gifts. It's much easier than it used to be for a woman to participate in politics and the sciences. Still, if you're a woman of action who's decisive and good at debate, the nicest thing some people will be able to say about you is that you're "strong." In American society, women can be smart as long as they're not aggressive, and yet there are times when our gifts embody so much power and drive that our very presence can overwhelm others. If your emotional make-up doesn't fit with society's idea of femininity—it's all right if you're strong, but please be sweet about it—you may get negative feedback. We can always learn to work with our emotions so that we express to others welcome, love, and acceptance. At the same time, we need to honor who we are, with all the equipment God gave us, and not worry so much about others' reactions.

The writer of Ephesians[16] says that God gives us gifts for building up the body of Christ. As we grow in friendship with God, we will see how every gift is a means of living God's love in the world. Whether we are writing stories or creating debt-relief programs in developing countries, our gifts are meant for good work, for forward movement. People who want to stay comfortable and not deal with the needs of others, people who prefer the status quo, will not be happy when our gifts are flourishing.

God has designed us to be energized through our giftedness. One of my favorite movie lines is from *Chariots of Fire*, when missionary and Olympic runner Eric Liddell says, in defense of his running, "God made me fast, and I feel God's pleasure when I run." What a liberating statement! Each of us should ask, *When do I feel God's pleasure?*

I remember when the Myers-Briggs personality indicator was first introduced into a particular mission organization. The organization began to make adjustments to job descriptions according to what the test revealed about missionaries' personalities. The immediate result was a remarkable spike in job satisfaction. Personnel counselors breathed a collective sigh of relief because they foresaw a much lower rate of burnout in the future. When people were assigned jobs that gave them energy rather than depleted it, morale in general rose and stress declined.

God's creation of us did not stop at bone structure and systems for respiration and circulation. Our very personality is a divine design. We are built to derive deep satisfaction from what our gifts enable us to accomplish. So it is no small thing to discover what gives us satisfaction and what we do particularly well.

If we spend enough time in the Room with God, we will begin to understand how divine love has been waiting for us to embrace our gifts rather than worry that they weren't the right gifts. When God meets our gifts with holy grace, divine love finds expression right in our lives, every day.

I loved to sway on the tire swing
on summer mornings when sunshine first
lit up the clover.
I loved riding my bike in the country
to smell crops greening or
gaze upon spider webs glistening.
I was quiet, liking to watch others and
listen to their conversations.
Blank paper excited me, along with
pretty journals, shiny pens.
You're saying that such things were
part of your Big Idea?
You're saying that you loved to watch me
love what I loved?
You're saying how deeply satisfying
to you is my deep satisfaction?
Does anyone else know this?

Here in the Room ☕

In whatever way works for you, talk to Jesus about your dearest loves. Name the interests and activities you have always enjoyed. Explain what you like to do when you have the luxury of unstructured time and no pressing tasks. Allow Jesus to explore with you the interests and activities that give you satisfaction and keep you motivated. Talk together about how you might better live out your gifts.

Name the negative pressures in your life associated with your loves and gifts.

If some of that pressure comes from other people, ask yourself these questions:

» Why is this person's opinion so important to me?

» What fear or resentment might be fueling this person's attitude toward my talents, interests, or personality traits?

» To what extent am I responsible for this person's level of comfort?

Gather a collection of one of the following: fruit, flowers, seashells, beautiful stones. These are symbols of your gifts. Arrange them in a bowl or on a tray. Bring this collection with you into the Room.

Now place your gifts before divine love. God the Father/Mother/Creator is here with you. Jesus is here. The Holy Spirit is here. In fact, the divine family is present—all the saints, along with angels, along with loved ones who have passed on. When you place your gifts here in the Room, you see around you a whole host that is your spiritual family.

You are sitting here with your gifts, but then you notice that everyone else is standing. You wonder why. Are you supposed to be standing, too? Are they expecting someone else?

But no. They are all standing and looking right at you. They aren't merely looking at you—they are beaming at you with such excitement and happiness that you still can't believe someone more important hasn't just walked in behind you. You turn around and, seeing no one else, know that all the smiles, all that focused attention, is on you.

Can you allow yourself to acknowledge what is happening now? Can you accept this grace? Not only are they all beaming at you, they are applauding. You, your gifts, your loves, are receiving a standing ovation. It's not the kind of ovation an audience gives when they feel it's the right thing to do. It's the response of your spiritual family to you—your willingness to own your giftedness, your openness to love what you love, your ability to move forward in your life whether or not others reward you for it.

This is an ovation of love. Stay right here and let it sink in.

CHAPTER 32

What can Jesus teach you about engagement?

Make me to know your ways, O LORD;
teach me your paths.
Lead me in your truth, and teach me,
for you are the God of my salvation;
for you I wait all day long.

Psalm 25:4–5

From ancient times, people of faith have engaged with the Divine through creative attentiveness to sacred stories. In its various forms this is known as *lectio divina* or spiritual reading. St. Ignatius developed this practice in his Spiritual Exercises, directing retreatants to engage their imaginations and their physical senses with various scenes in the life of Jesus.

If we pay close attention to what we read in Scripture about Jesus, and if we infuse that attention with imagination, we can begin to perceive him as a real person who had to deal with life as any human being must. For instance, when, at age twelve, Jesus traveled with his parents to the temple in Jerusalem, he got involved in lengthy discussions with some of the scholars and clergy-types there. His insight impressed them, and they all became so engrossed that Jesus lingered even after his family had headed back to Nazareth; Mary and Joseph had to come find him. Of course they were upset with their son, but it was obvious that young Jesus had just entered a new realm of spirituality, a new stage in his personal inward journey. He had found a place for his passion and his hunger for God. I imagine it as a great opening within him, as his spiritual awareness merged with the confirmation he found in sharing his insights with these much older men trained in Torah.

There is no way Jesus' life simply returned to normal after that. The Scriptures say that he went home and was obedient to his parents. But don't you think Mary and Joseph had some serious discussions about how they could best nurture these gifts in their son? I can imagine Joseph going to the local rabbi and arranging for Jesus to spend more time in study, so that his youthful insights could have mentoring and direction.

Then there were the years between ages twelve and thirty, when Jesus worked alongside his father, doing carpentry. We have to wonder how Jesus, Mary, and Joseph determined what Jesus would do and how. Did he, or they, hope he could train to become a rabbi? Did his study remain private, perhaps through mentoring relationships with more than one teacher, with men who could train him in prayer and meditation? No one knows, but something was happening all those years to prepare him for the three years of intense ministry that would culminate in his destiny as Savior of the world.

Then came the day when he knew it was time to walk out the door, a moment every one of us has experienced. Jesus knew he must go to his cousin John (the locust-eating preacher) and get baptized. And then—as much as I imagine he wanted to stay around John, perhaps even join John in ministry or become his disciple—Jesus felt compelled to walk right out into wilderness and spiritual hardship, a forty-day fast. Again, such things don't simply happen; we work up to them, spend time praying and doing our best to discern the next step.

In fact, we can follow Jesus' story and know that he learned, day by day, to nourish his own gifts, listen to divine wisdom in his own heart, spend hours and hours with God in conversation, walk from this place to the next one, deal with each situation as it arrived, encounter people he expected and many he didn't, fight battles he didn't start, love people as best he knew, help others through sheer intuition and common sense . . . In other words, Jesus walked through his life much as we must walk through ours, making choices and saying yes to God one day at a time.

Jesus engaged with the life he'd been given. He took his gifts into every day and offered them to divine power and purpose. My definition of gifts here is quite broad. There are natural talents as well as acquired skills. There are spiritual gifts or sensitivities as well as a particular configuration of experiences. Jesus' divine nature aside, he had gifts of a Jewish lineage, a spiritually sensitive mother, and a generous, ethical father. His early history in Egypt, along with his years in the Galilee region, added to the equipment Jesus had for engaging with life. His gifts included his own spiritual hunger, dating back at least to age twelve and probably much earlier. His apprenticeship in carpentry was yet another aspect of giftedness. Scripture does not say how he nurtured his spiritual abilities through those years of carpentry, but he certainly didn't neglect them, or he would not have been able to step onto the road of baptism, wilderness fast, and demanding ministry. Here was not simply a young man God had chosen to drag a cross through Jerusalem at a key moment in history. Here was a boy, a teenager, a son, a student, a tradesman, and finally a teacher, a healer, a spiritual companion, a Savior, who consistently chose to participate with God through the means at hand.

While we certainly don't claim the same gifts and situations as those that were given to Jesus, God asks no more and no less of us than what was required of Jesus. The question is, will we engage, or won't we? Will we use whatever gifts we have, or will we hold back and resist the very powers and abilities we possess?

By now I've referred numerous times to our being in the Room with God, but perhaps I've misled you to think that we spend most of that time sitting around. Jesus' story shows us that our friendship with God will lead to ever more engagement with life. Think about your best human relationships. Don't they often lead you into passionate activity? Don't you *do* things with friends—explore ideas, come up with plans, feel even more empowered to change the world?

As you grow in friendship with God, God will not allow you to stay in one place or be comfortable for long. Through your gifts, passions, desires, and abilities, God will compel you right into your life—just as Jesus was compelled to go from one town to the next. Like any good friend, God will not allow you to dismiss your gifts and get lazy. God will use those very gifts to engage you with what divine love is doing in the world.

God works through our gifts and also through our circumstances, whether or not we have freely chosen them. Of course we wish some aspects of our life had been different. I would have preferred to marry younger so that I could have had children. I sometimes catch myself wishing for a different educational background, particularly when it comes to my writing life. I'm sure that the teenage Jesus considered more than once how much more he could have nurtured his scholarly, spiritual gifts if his father were a scholar or scribe and not a tradesman. Or how wonderful it would have been to live in Jerusalem, where he would have had so much more access to the teachers in the temple, rather than in a distant village. But Jesus' unique history prepared him to live a unique story in the world, and your history has done the same for you. It is through the energy of divine friendship that you can work with your life rather than against it.

---

*My flight was delayed by hours and so I
managed another one on another
carrier, which meant another set of
passengers—different people sitting next to
me, different flight attendants;
we landed at a different time*

and I rented a different car, which meant
that I was on the road with different drivers
and drove through intersections at a different
time, and I ate dinner much later
though at probably the same restaurant.
Actually, because it was later, they'd run out
of the special, and I chatted not with other
supper customers but with four police
officers, themselves grabbing a late meal—
God only knows how many times
their day had shifted orbit.
And wouldn't it be a huge, sad shame
if any of us had decided not to enjoy
any part of this day—the high clouds,
the late food, the conversation—because
we considered it not really our life
but only a digression?

Here in the Room

What has prepared you for the life you are now living? Let's break that question into smaller pieces:

» How did your upbringing enhance your ability to engage with life as it really is?

» What did parents, neighbors, friends, relatives, teachers, and others instill in you that has helped you make good choices or determine how to handle situations?

» What desires have been burning in you since childhood? What hungers have lived within you from earliest memory?

» List the jobs you've had—even the bad ones. What emotional or spiritual or mental or vocational skills developed out of those experiences?

» Name the painful experiences in your life up until now. Try to think of one good thing that has formed in you because of each experience—even if the only thing worth mentioning is that you proved to yourself you could survive horror and devastation.

» What roles have you played in family life? How have you been shaped by being a daughter, sister, girlfriend, lover, wife, mother, aunt, grandmother?

» What functions have you served in systems of relationships? Caregiver? Supervisor? Cheerleader? Wise woman? Mediator? Facilitator?

Jesus' life had several pivotal moments (unusual birth, temple experience at age twelve, baptism, forty days of prayer and fasting in the wilderness, and so on). We have our own histories of pivotal moments, each launching us to a new level of engagement with our gifts, with our situations, and with our relationship to God.

Invite Jesus to sit with you now, in the Room. Talk with him about the similarities between his life and yours. Talk about the differences. Tell Jesus how you feel about your own history.

---- CHAPTER 33 ----

How does the Holy Spirit engage with you?

You have turned my mourning into dancing;
you have taken off my sackcloth
and clothed me with joy,
so that my soul may praise you and not
be silent.
O LORD my God, I will give thanks to
you forever.

Psalm 30:11–12

When I was about twenty and first teaching, I got caught in a collision of three relationships. Looking back on it, I can say that I did nothing immoral or unethical. The worst I did was try to help too much, and I repeated one comment someone had said, in hopes of helping another person better understand that person's position. And the second person repeated what I had said to the third person, only changed a key word, which made the statement quite inflammatory. I didn't know at the time that any such thing was happening; I was involved with the three different people in three different contexts. They were connected to one another in a strange configuration of their own.

One morning, while I was driving to my work, I had a strong sense about these three people. There was no audible voice, but I know it was the Holy Spirit, my constant alongside-friend, saying, in essence, that all hell was about to break loose. Sure enough, when I arrived at the school, a discussion occurred that tore me apart. I realized that my words had been twisted and that now three people were very angry with me. I knew I had done nothing wrong, that in fact a lack of integrity in at least one of those people and simple thoughtlessness in another was at the root of this mess. I remember thinking, *The Holy Spirit told me this would happen. Just relax; this is outside your control.* And, although I was very hurt by this experience, I sensed within myself a calm that enabled me to keep on with my teaching and stay in communication with all three people.

> *And I will ask the Father, and he will give you another Advocate, to be with you forever. This is the Spirit of truth, whom the world cannot receive, because it neither sees him nor knows him. You know him, because he abides with you, and he will be in you.*
>
> —John 14:16–17

Throughout this book I've referred to entering the Room— one way of being intentional about dwelling with God. The Room is a simple image because we all know what a room is, and we understand the dynamics of walking through a door to be with someone. We have imagined being with God in the Room in several ways. We have imagined Jesus sitting in the Room with us. I think, though, that when we consider the Holy Spirit, it's more like the Room being inside us.

The Holy Spirit living in us is a crucial aspect of the reciprocal relationship between us and divine love. When Jesus was here in person, his friends could be with him and he with them. He knew that humans are not very adept at maintaining relationship long-distance, without a tangible presence to relate to. So he told his friends that, although he would leave them, he would send another, the Holy Spirit. This happened fifty days after the first Easter, on the day of Pentecost.

When the Holy Spirit arrived, the friends of Jesus who had been hiding ever since the crucifixion, fearing the political and religious leaders, were suddenly walking anywhere and everywhere, talking about Jesus, proclaiming God's presence. These fishermen and other ordinary folk had acquired miraculous confidence in who Jesus was and what he had accomplished. The Holy Spirit gave them words to say and the courage to say them, stayed with them when they got thrown into prison, and enabled some of them to die bravely later on, when Rome got nervous about so many friends of Jesus running around upsetting things.

God-within-us provides what we need to endure anything. Sometimes we endure horrible abuse, sometimes long years of illness or financial stress. We may endure fractured marriages and estranged children or parents. We may endure oppression in its many forms, whether we are poor, a minority, female, or too young to fight for ourselves. Like the early Christians, we need the Holy Spirit's help; and like them, we can receive it.

This presence is what enables us to move through any situation with grace. Often we go through something and later wonder how we managed it. We can't see how we prepared to do what we did, or how we had the energy, imagination, or fortitude to do what we did. That's because there was more than our own energy, imagination, or fortitude at work.

The tough reality is that we must endure struggle. It is woven through our days like a thread in fabric; to yank out the struggle is to unravel the life. That struggle thread is part of what strengthens the whole. As we walk through our days and nights, we work the struggle thread into the general weave of things.

All of this sounds rather out there, philosophical and poetic. What does it really mean to me when I'm trying to get an unauthorized withdrawal stricken from my bank account so that I won't be overdrawn by several hundred dollars for another week? Or when I let my adult child move home, knowing she's back on drugs but hoping against hope I can convince her to go into treatment again? Or when the man who used to love me is now torturing and bankrupting me through a drawn-out divorce process? What does it mean during these times to be friends with the Divine? Here are three true statements to consider.

We are not alone. A true friend stays with us through hell. That friend may sit next to us and not say a word, because there's nothing to say. But his or her presence gives us strength and comfort. Because God is our friend and the Holy Spirit dwells in the Room that is our life, we will face nothing absolutely alone.

The truth is preserved. We are often most hurt, as I was with my three friends, by people believing falsehoods about us. One of the most insidious aspects of messy divorces is how two people are encouraged—usually by their attorneys—to reinvent history and turn each other into monsters they never were, for the sake of getting more money or a larger share of the children's custody. I've seen women and men completely devastated because their children were convinced by the other parent that Mommy didn't take good care of them or that Daddy wouldn't give them any money. Truth is not simply a legal matter; it is deeply moral and spiritual, and we suffer great pain when people think falsely of us. Just as we rely on the one or two friends who will always know the truth and stick up for us, we can trust that God will hold forever the truth of who we are. When everyone else believes the lie, all heaven will maintain the truth.

There is always the next thing to do. Because, in divine life, we are already on the other side of the temporary, physical realm of suffering, we can set our sights beyond the present situation. I don't mean by that an obsession with heaven, although some days it's a comfort to believe that this life isn't all there is, that ultimately we will rest with God, free of trouble and pain. And I don't mean that we gloss over the bad that's happening or minimize it or spiritualize it to the point that we don't deal with it. But even while we live on a conflicted planet, we can think forward. We can, with the Holy Spirit's help, keep imagining and planning how to express God's love in the current situation.

Where did so many social reforms originate during the eighteenth and nineteenth centuries—such as public education, women's rights, labor laws, humane treatment of criminals and the mentally ill, and the abolition of slavery? Most of them were started by Christians who saw horrendous circumstances and did what they were convinced God wanted done. Who are some of the most hopeful, active people you meet today? They work with AIDS patients or in hospices, or out in the streets with the homeless, or on war-torn continents bringing provisions and setting up microenterprises. In the most depressing circumstances, the Holy Spirit generates hope, resourcefulness, energy, and creativity. When we carry around the Room inside us, we become factories for these things.

Much struggle awaits us, but everything that happens is raw material for the Holy Spirit. For God's friends, conflict is just one more means of bearing fruit. When we realize this and believe it, we are free to see reality for what it is. Being God's friend doesn't mean that I say things are fine when they aren't, but that I acknowledge the constant possibility for transformation, change, and redemption. Carrying the Room within me increases my own capacity to endure the hard parts of life. I can admit when I hurt or suffer great loss, because I know that, here in the Room, my resources are still endless.

Some days I would really like for things
to really work out—no offense,
but belief isn't enough; hope isn't enough.
To be blunt, truth isn't enough either.
I need to be relieved, or to be believed.
So what will You do? Where are You?
Appear, please,
and straighten out this world.
Well, as usual, You take my words,
my dreams, and play little tricks,
and grab me from behind and we twirl
through reasons and confusions
and settle down to watch a spider
create her tiny wheel of air and thread.
While she spins, ignoring us,
we argue about options, then sigh heavily
and find something to eat.
After awhile, we sleep out our exhaustion,
then wake up to sirens, and sun on the floor,
and realize only then
that we have a plan
and all the time in the world.

Here in the Room 🍵_____

Enter a time of quiet. Take several deep breaths and clear the clutter from your thoughts. Then enter this story:

You are walking through very rough terrain. There are large rocks to climb over or around, deep muddy ruts, and thickets to get through. Inside the thickets, the air is close and hot. Up on the hard, exposed ridges, the wind chills you. You look ahead and see mile upon mile of this environment to navigate.

After a day or two of this, you become aware of another person on the path with you. She is quiet but friendly. She's energetic as she walks, and her arms and legs are strong and fit. She walks close to you, and when you slip or falter, one of those steady arms reaches for you. When the temperature falls and the wind kicks up, she pulls you close and the two of you form a shelter with your bodies. As the hours go by, you take turns finding pools to drink from, or fruit to eat.

At one point you are so weary and full of aches and bruises that all you can do is sit in the mud and cry. Your companion sits there with you, stays while the tears flow and the angry words fly from your mouth. She doesn't say anything, but you feel intense care radiating from her to you.

Finally, you get through the long miles and land in a better place. People have been waiting for you and applaud as you walk through the door. Your friend comes in as well. You tell the others that you might not have made it if it hadn't been for this friend. They are impressed, but she is happy to find a seat and have a cup of coffee. She says it was no big deal; this is what friends do. As you are leaving the party, you notice that she's still sitting there, content to share in the moment. She's so quiet that you almost left without her. But you ask if she'd like to come along, and she says of course—life is a long adventure to be shared with others.

What did it feel like, to discover a friend on this journey?

If you could ask this person any questions you wanted, what would they be?

If you want to go a little deeper . . .

Create your own story about the Holy Spirit. Go on a journey or complete a dangerous task or face someone who is angry with you—do anything at all, but be sure to include a character or some other presence representing the Holy Spirit. Describe that presence and your reaction to it.

CHAPTER 34

How do you choose a way and follow it?

> I bless the LORD who gives me counsel;
>> in the night also my heart instructs me.
> I keep the Lord always before me;
>> because he is at my right hand, I shall not
>>> be moved. . . .
> You show me the path of life.
>> In your presence there is fullness of joy;
>> in your right hand are pleasures forevermore.
>
> Psalm 16:7–8, 11

To be engaged is to be in motion. Although our engagement with God will sometimes involve stillness—meditation, contemplation, listening, rest—it is not passive. The universe as God designed it is not static but dynamic, which is what we're meant to be. Anyone who has experienced a lengthy hospital stay or who has been put on sustained bed rest during a difficult pregnancy understands that passivity gets old very quickly. Most of us want to keep moving. The question is, where? The problem usually is not passivity but paralysis. We're not sure which way to go or how to get there.

Many years ago I heard this statement in a taped sermon by Peter Lord, a Florida pastor: "You can choose the road you take, but you cannot choose where that road takes you." Those words have fortified me many times as I've negotiated the spiritual life. I remind myself that the road I chose was friendship with God. Once I made that choice, many other decisions were automatically determined for me, decisions about how I would conduct myself and what my priorities would be. In walking alongside Jesus, I am gradually learning to live as he lived, to go about my life peacefully, faithfully, generously, truthfully. My overall commitment to this relationship with the Divine should ultimately shape all my other choices.

But within the larger choices about what kind of person I'm going to be are innumerable other, subtler choices about what I'll do this hour or say to this person. Also, there are not-so-subtle choices that involve picking one of several good options, such as where to go to college or which job to accept or which person to date or what city to live in.

This topic of decision making, sometimes called *discernment*, fills many books. I offer just a few good principles. Each of these appears in some form in the *Spiritual Exercises* of St. Ignatius, and all of them have emerged in various other systems, from Eastern religions to American business books.[17]

» Make lists of pros and cons for each option. This simple exercise is especially effective when the lists turn out to be significantly lopsided, showing one option to be much better or worse than the other.

» Pay attention to desolation and consolation. The Holy Spirit within you is informing your hunches, desires, and emotions. Allow yourself to dwell in those dynamics and learn from them.

» Beware of harmful attachments. The most clearheaded decisions are made when we are not compelled by desperation or avoidance. If possible, bring yourself to the point of being comfortable with either option.

» Counsel yourself as you would counsel another person who is facing the same decision you are facing. This can provide enough emotional distance for you to see more clearly.

» Imagine that you are at the end of your life, looking back. What decision do you wish you had made concerning the present issue? On your deathbed, what would emerge as the right thing to do or the most important step to take?

And if you still aren't completely sure what to do, do something anyway. Ask God to throw in a roadblock if you're heading in the wrong direction. Sometimes you have to get onto a certain road because, although you don't know it, there's another road leading off this one, and that other road is the one you need to get to. So God uses your desire or the situation that has put you on this road to get you to the crucial intersection that is still miles from here.

God, who is your friend, will not be angry if you land on the wrong road. As long as you're moving, divine love can redirect your steps or stop you inches from danger. But if you stay stuck out of fear or indecision, well, it's hard to steer a parked car. It isn't in God's nature to force us to do things. Friendship guides, it does not coerce. Divine love is waiting for your next step, whatever it is.

Well, I just don't know.
I hate making decisions—
they rearrange everything, and
I've finally gotten comfortable with the
last configuration that is my life.
Can't we just cruise for a while?
Can't I decide not to decide?
What if this doesn't work?
What if—oh my—what if I'm wrong?
I'd rather let someone else decide, really.
I'm happy to go along with whatever
the rest of you want to do. Yes, let me
ride along. I'll sit in the back seat
and not say a word.
And when we get lost and everyone just
wants a hot meal and a clean bed,
I'll remind you that this wasn't my idea.

Here in the Room

What is most difficult for you when it comes to making decisions?

If you can, remember a time when you seemed to be on the wrong road but somehow things worked out anyway. What happened exactly, and how did you respond?

Who have been the major decision makers in your personal history? In your family of origin, who made the decisions? Who has had that role in your marriage? Or, if you're single, how do you make decisions and whom—if anyone—do you rely on for help?

If there's a decision you need to make now, whether it's major or minor, use one or more of the principles listed in the chapter. Later, reflect on what that experience was like.

CHAPTER 35

How do joy and gratitude nourish your friendship?

*Make a joyful noise to the L*ORD*, all the earth.*
*Worship the L*ORD *with gladness;*
come into his presence with singing.
*Know that the L*ORD *is God.*
It is he that made us, and we are his;
we are his people, and the sheep of
his pasture.

Psalm 100:1–3

Just about everyone in my family of origin has a green thumb except for me. My father—who could grow anything and had great intuition as a gardener—used to bring me live plants when he and Mom came to visit. And with each visit he brought hardier and hardier plants, because somehow I managed to kill everything through my great striving to nurture.

Years later, when my husband and I moved to a house with a bit of yard, I embarked upon an awakening that occurred in at least two stages. We moved here in the dead of winter, and my initial stage of tending green things was to watch them sprout up in the yard come spring and to begin identifying them. The bright blades of lilies popped through the gray soil, and I did a little dance in front of them—my gosh, I'd have actual flowers in my yard! Then there were tiny blue flowers all over the lawn, and wild onions in one corner near the alley. And the trees leafed out, and I identified their names. After living three stories up with only a porch facing the alley, I expressed what may have seemed to others an inordinate level of joy over grass coming up.

Stage two was to plant things and hope they would survive. The first spring we put in a tiny garden, and angels stood by to protect the tomatoes, basil, and lettuce from my incompetence. My joy increased tenfold a couple of months later when I harvested ripe tomatoes and my own herbs. It occurred to me that possibly I could grow things and not kill them. I'm sure that coworkers were amused at my great enthusiasm when in the lunchroom I celebrated quite vocally my very own home-grown tomatoes. But between angelic intervention and my husband's knowledge and experience, we enjoyed our garden well into the autumn, finishing with green-tomato relish.

I can honestly say that I meet God when pulling ripe tomatoes off the vine. The joy of this participation in nature now triggers my enjoyment of God's love. This is a spiritual habit—to connect everyday joy with eternal God. We can learn this joy in several arenas.

Joy in creation. We are more inclined to experience joy when witnessing something extraordinary, such as the Grand Canyon, an island paradise, or a luxurious snowfall. We forget that ordinary weather is creation as well and that green grass emerging in a cluttered city is its own miracle. Thus, we can murmur praise when the air is clear and the sun bright; we can take pleasure in a long, soaking rain and the soft glow of twilight. We can say thank you for a breeze or snowflakes, for clouds that pile up like mountains or spread across the sky like fine silk. I praise God for birds at the feeder, for my furry pets lounging around me, for the fishy aroma of Lake Michigan at certain times of the year. Anyone can revel in good weather, but a friend of the Divine has a name for the loving force behind all of humming, shining nature. And so when we pause to enjoy the created world, we can say, "Thank you, God."

Joy in immediate experience. Religions of an Eastern mindset have been adept at helping people learn to take joy in the present moment. Christian spirituality values this ability too, but the Western mindset is so focused upon productivity that even in our blissful moments we are likely to be planning a next step or trying to formulate some kind of rational system in which to place our bliss.

How often are you able to enjoy fully what you are presently doing—without thinking back to what you've already done or ahead to what you hope to do? We miss a lot of joy that is right in front of us, every day. We eat a good meal, have a pleasant conversation with a friend or colleague. We are able to get up and move around without pain or great fatigue. We know how to do things—run machinery, throw parties, create works of art, enjoy the complex series of movements and thoughts involved in a simple game of softball. We stroke our cats and dogs, laugh at movies, sing songs (in harmony!), debate with one another, paint and decorate rooms or entire houses. We find relief for pain, and we solve problems. We have sex and nurture our various emotional and spiritual attachments to other persons. We make money and spend money. We help others and receive help.

And yet . . . as we move through the hours and days, so often our attention is not on the present movement but on something else—a worry or a regret or a plan. We mute our awareness of this moment in favor of being anxious about moments that have not arrived. Or we are too distracted by what has already happened to notice fully what is happening now.

Joy in work well done. In the story of the Garden of Eden, human beings had work to do from the first days of Paradise. The coming of sin changed the nature of work to something hard and toilsome, but we were created to thrive through working. In fact, we have the ability to experience deep joy and satisfaction in our work.

I've been a working writer for more than a decade, but it took me about five years to learn that it was all right to rejoice upon the publication of a book. At one point I remarked to a friend, "No matter where you are in the process of a book, there is some anxiety attached. First, you're anxious that no publisher will offer a contract. Once you have the contract, you worry about fulfilling it satisfactorily. Once you've turned the manuscript over to the editor, you worry that he or she will find horrible, unfixable flaws in it. Once it's in proofreading, you worry that the readers will find yet more embarrassing flaws and convince the editors to rethink the whole thing. Once the book is in print, you worry about what the reviewers will say. And once it's on bookshelves, you worry that it won't sell." I had managed to put off joy at every stage of the process.

Yet as I paid better attention to my creative process and to God's voice in my heart—and as I listened to a good friend who took me to task—it became clear that my tendency to push past the finished work was not so much modesty as ingratitude.

Joy in relationships. When we appreciate and enjoy human relationships, we are enjoying God's presence. God smiles at us on the bus, amuses us at the mall, astounds us in the concert hall. When we maintain relationship with other people, we offer them our strength, wisdom, and support, and they offer the same to us. This may sound simple and self-evident, but many of us feel as if we have failed when we need someone's help. We don't want that interdependence. Our resistance toward God is often manifested in our resistance toward other people—our unwillingness to be part of community, to receive help, or to offer our own abundance to serve others' needs.

Nearly two decades of marriage have taught me that relationship is far more than the sum of two people added together. The relationship itself has its own character, rhythm, and pattern of growth. The relationship is not just a matter of how Jim treats me or of how I treat him; it is the constant merging of our two lives into a flow of emotion, commitment, desire, discernment, action, and reflection. I enter each day as a participant in this flow, not as someone wanting her needs to be met, and not as someone responsible for meeting another person's needs. I can take joy in being in this relationship, even when I cannot make Jim happy today or solve all his problems. I can receive his love today knowing that his love won't be enough to satisfy my complicated mixture of wants and whims. No, we aren't enough for each other, but that's not really the point. We have entered this life together, and the life itself will lead us—as all good things lead us—into God's constant embrace. Because of this, I can experience joy on good days and bad days.

Joy in natural human processes. Since turning forty a decade ago, I have had to learn about natural process. I've been forced to pay better attention to what my body needs, as hormonal shifts created new demands and a different sort of balance. My initial response to such change was dismay if not outright anger. Because my view of the body has been so influenced by Western medicine, I still tend to think of my physical systems as machines that must be controlled or repaired. Only during the past few years have I entertained the notion that I can take joy in the processes of midlife change. If I can let go of the idea that I must control this body and conquer its every upheaval, then I am freer to take joy in all this chemistry and organic change, which occurs miraculously and in its own time.

Other, less tumultuous processes give us the opportunity to entertain joy and gratitude. Rather than get irritated when we're hungry, we could consider hunger simply part of the cycle whereby we receive nourishment, use up the energy it provides, then find nourishment again. Thus a growling stomach is anticipation of the meal that's coming—and it's also a built-in warning system that ensures I eat and keep living. The same with the process of work and rest. Who hasn't taken joy in the exhaustion that follows a day of working in the yard or preparing for a major event? Why not consider it joy when we can shower off the grime and fall into bed? We usually don't struggle to enjoy the tension-release cycle of sexuality, with its flirtation, build-up, and climax; we know (or learn) how to enjoy the tension leading to release. We practice joy and gratitude when we embrace these various natural cycles of being human.

Imagine that you give a gift to a good friend, but she is too distracted to really look at it—in fact, she barely acknowledges it. Perhaps she says a perfunctory thank-you, but you do not feel that she has connected with you or the gift. Not only are you hurt by this but you're also frustrated to see that even though this gift was just right for her, she's not enjoying it at all. If she would simply allow herself to receive this gift, the joy would be there for her. And if she truly received the gift, she'd throw her arms around you with multiple thank-yous. That would be a friendship kind of engagement. That would be true connection.

Here in the Room

Create a physical space in your life, in which you can focus on, and enjoy, creation. It could be a single potted plant or window box, a bird feeder, a window that gives a great view of the evening or morning sky. Try to involve all of your senses as you receive and appreciate what God has given you.

Go through a day—or through a single hour—and discipline yourself to attend to each moment as it comes and to note what is praiseworthy in that moment. Try to build this habit of dwelling completely in the moment at hand rather than in the past or future.

Identify some task you have accomplished and come up with a little celebration of it. This can be private or with friends.

Write a poem about one of your significant relationships. Make it a poem of wonder and praise.

Choose a natural process to enter more intentionally. You might try eating much more slowly and mindfully, thoroughly tasting the food. Or you could notice, over the next few nights, what your process is like for falling asleep. Allow yourself to enjoy the natural tension and release of ordinary processes in your life.

PART EIGHT

Love

God, I give you the praise for days well spent. But I am yet unsatisfied, because I do not enjoy enough of you. I apprehend myself at too great a distance from you. I would have my soul more closely united to you by faith and love. You know Lord that I would love you above all things. You made me, you know my desires, my expectations. My joys all center in you and it is you that I desire. It is your favor, your acceptance, the communications of your grace that I earnestly wish for more than anything in the world. I rejoice in your essential glory and blessedness. I rejoice in my relation to you, that you are my Father, my Lord and my God. I thank you that you have brought me so far.

SUSANNA WESLEY[18]

Human beings possess an astounding capacity to love, and the power unleashed when we give ourselves freely to love is so intense that we sometimes shy away from love rather than embrace it. We know that passionate love has the power to transform whomever it touches.

A woman's potential to love has always been a primary source of her power. We did not own the property, make the rules, control commerce, or determine how justice would be applied. We did not write the books or map the courses of most civil institutions. Yet we loved mightily. We have loved God and God's world through listening, heeding wisdom, using our imagination, nurturing others, and following our passion. Our love has changed history.

The chapters of this final part of the book focus on women who loved God. Their encounters with the Divine reveal how we can offer God our friendship at its most beautiful and most powerful.

CHAPTER 36

How does listening express love?

For God alone my soul waits in silence;
from him comes my salvation. . . .
Once God has spoken;
twice have I heard this:
that power belongs to God,
and steadfast love belongs to you, O Lord.
For you repay to all
according to their work.

Psalm 62:1, 11–12

In present-day north Jordan, a land that's part of the bibli-cal Palestine where Jesus once walked and preached, several young churches thrive. They did not exist back in the 1950s, but some women started getting together at one another's homes, to visit and pray and learn about the Bible. The visit is paramount in Arab culture; the nomadic code of giving hospitality to strangers long ago evolved into lavish rituals of sharing numerous courses of food and drink while talking of family, current events, and anything else of interest. And so, in the context of this leisurely interaction, churches were born. It started with the women, doing what women have always known how to do: talk and listen and share sustenance.

Let's look now at another visit, in a story we have heard many times.

> Now as they went on their way, he entered a certain village, where a woman named Martha welcomed him into her home. She had a sister named Mary, who sat at the Lord's feet and listened to what he was saying. But Martha was distracted by her many tasks; so she came to him and asked, "Lord, do you not care that my sister has left me to do all the work by myself? Tell her then to help me." But the Lord answered her, "Martha, Martha, you are worried and distracted by many things; there is need of only one thing. Mary has chosen the better part, which will not be taken away from her."
>
> —Luke 10:38–42

We've probably heard numerous lessons and homilies about the differences between these two sisters—the one who worked hard and the other who devoted herself to Jesus' teaching. I grew up having the question posed to me by preachers and teachers: "Are you going to be a Martha, or a Mary?" as if only one of them found favor with Jesus. Each woman had a place in this story, and you'll notice that Martha was the one who welcomed Jesus into their home in the first place. But Mary is the focus of our thoughts now.

Many biblical scholars consider Mary a disciple. She "sat at the Lord's feet," a phrase usually applied to a disciple, who sat at the feet of the teacher. That Mary sat at Jesus' feet was no indication of her place as a woman but a clear statement that Jesus was teaching her. The *New Revised Standard Version* commentary on this verse says simply, "This was exceptional for women."

In John 11:5, we read that "Jesus loved Martha and her sister and Lazarus." He showed up at their home more than once, giving the general impression that these women and their brother were friends of his. I imagine that in their home he could relax and not only be welcomed as teacher but enjoy what others gave him, whether their food or their company. But when I read this story a few months ago during prayerful retreat, another phrase stood out: Mary "listened to what he was saying." She listened to Jesus, and I don't think it was merely listening to get spiritual enlightenment or information. I believe Mary's sort of listening was in the category of loving attention.

We are accustomed to thinking in terms of what Jesus gave to the people around him. But what did they give to him? He called them his friends, and we know that true friendship goes both ways. We also know that one of the most crucial ways a good friend loves us is by simply listening to us.

We are desperate to be heard, truly heard, by the people who love us. Sometimes we need to talk awhile, to let out what's on our heart in the presence of someone who cares enough to sit with us and help us sort through our words and thoughts. Listening expresses so many things: respect, empathy, trust, interest, care. And Mary listened to Jesus—not just because Jesus was a wise teacher but because Jesus was a friend, and because Jesus, just like any other human being, needed friends who would truly listen to him.

Recall his adventure with the elders in the temple, back when he was twelve. Probably he had been waiting for just that kind of audience to hear him express what he was learning about the Scriptures and about God. Suddenly there they were, these learned men, and they were gracious enough and kind enough to listen to this boy talk out what was happening inside him. What a gift that was to a boy on the cusp of spiritual pilgrimage.

How many times did that sort of generous listening really happen for Jesus? Of course his disciples listened to him, and the crowds listened, but they listened out of need and questioning. As a workshop leader, I feel a keen difference between the listening that happens when I'm instructing and the listening I receive from a friend. We know what it's like to sit up late and just talk, to let our ideas tumble around and have others work with them, to have others hear us and help us struggle toward what we're trying to figure out.

We can't know for certain what was happening when Mary sat at Jesus' feet, so engaged that her sister couldn't drag her away. But I believe Mary was loving Jesus as a friend loves, by listening patiently, maintaining openness in posture and facial expression, and conveying an attitude of acceptance and affection.

Yes, listening is a form of love, and as we befriend the Divine we can express our love through an act of generous attention. We listen to God when we listen to other people with care and grace. We listen to God by sitting with the sacred stories and allowing them to sink in a little further. We listen to God by

Here in the Room ☕

Recall the last time someone listened to you without looking at their watch. How did that level of attentiveness affect you?

Sit with another person (friend, colleague) during your lunch hour or coffee break. Ask that person a question, and do not interject any other question or statement while he or she is talking. While that person is talking, drag yourself away from the temptation to plan what you will say next. Note what it feels like to listen so actively and completely to another.

Reread the Scripture passage about Mary and Jesus.

Now, imagine you are Mary, here in this present Room, and Jesus is sitting across from you. He's tired from his work, enjoying food and drink, catching up with what's happening in your life. After a while he begins to talk, and talk. And you fasten yourself to him and all that he is saying. From time to time, you respond to his thoughts. The two of you sit, and the words keep coming, and time slides by.

Write down the conversation, or speak it into a recorder.

CHAPTER 37

Why does your wisdom matter?

I will instruct you and teach you the way you
 should go;
 I will counsel you with my eye upon you.
Do not be like a horse or a mule, without
 understanding,
 whose temper must be curbed with bit
  and bridle,
 else it will not stay near you.

Psalm 32:8–9

In her memoir, *A Border Passage*, Leila Ahmed makes a fascinating observation about Islam, the faith of her Egyptian upbringing.

> The women had . . . their own understanding of Islam,
> an understanding that was different from men's Islam,

"official" Islam. . . . It was through religion that one
pondered the things that happened, why they had happened, and what one should make of them, how one
should take them.

Islam, as I got it from [the women], was gentle,
generous, pacifist, inclusive, somewhat mystical—just
as they themselves were. . . . Religion was above all
about inner things. The outward signs of religiousness,
such as prayer and fasting, might be signs of a true
religiousness but equally well might not. They were
certainly not what was important about being Muslim.
What was important was how you conducted yourself and how you were in yourself and in your attitude
toward others and in your heart.[19]

She goes on to describe how, for men, Islam was learned
from the classic texts as taught by mullahs and sheiks, how it
formed the worship inside mosques, and how it was, in general, what the world typically knew as Islam. Because women in
Middle Eastern countries had, until recent history, been illiter-
ate and not allowed to attend worship at the mosques or hear the
teaching directly, their take on religion had formed differently.

[Women] figured these things out among themselves
. . . as they tried to understand their own lives and how
to behave and how to live, talking them over together
among themselves, interacting with their men, and
returning to talk them over in their communities of

women. And they figured them out as they listened to the Quran and talked among themselves about what they had heard. . . . There was merit in having the Quran chanted in your house and in listening to it being chanted wherever it was chanted, whereas for women there was no merit attached to attending mosque, an activity indeed prohibited to women for most of history.

As I read Ahmad's description of her faith tradition, some lights went on concerning my own. Certainly Christianity has always had its "male" and "female" sides, going clear back to its Judaic roots. Certainly the way women absorb and process spiritual information continues to be different from how men—and patriarchal cultures—deal with spirituality.

Perhaps one advantage of women's being marginalized for so long in areas of government, business, and academia is that we have been free to carry on in areas of intuition, dream, and vision without much interference. Perhaps our wisdom was not taken seriously ("old wives' tales"), but we have never completely lost touch with that deeply spiritual side of life.

In the Gospel of Matthew, I believe we see a woman's intuition at work.

Now while Jesus was at Bethany in the house of Simon the leper, a woman came to him with an alabaster jar of very costly ointment, and she poured it on his head as he sat at the table. But when the disciples saw it, they were angry and said, "Why this waste? For this ointment could have been sold for a large sum, and the money given to the poor." But Jesus, aware of this, said to them, "Why do you trouble the woman? She has performed a good service for me. For you always have the poor with you, but you will not always have me. By pouring this ointment on my body she has prepared me for burial. Truly I tell you, wherever this good news is proclaimed in the whole world, what she has done will be told in remembrance of her."

—Matthew 26:6–13

What compelled this woman to break into a room full of men and commit such an extravagant act? A person didn't just anoint someone in this fashion every day. In fact, the particulars of this anointing point to two possible motivations. Such expensive ointment was used to prepare a body for burial, so it's possible that she anointed Jesus because she knew his death was imminent. The fact that she anointed his head could mean that she was proclaiming to all present that he was indeed the king, the long-awaited Messiah, because such anointing had marked that sort of announcement since Old Testament days when a prophet would anoint the person God had chosen to be king.

By this point in Jesus' ministry, he had said more than once that he was going to be put to death. But the disciples didn't hear him. The men who had lived with him and worked with him could not let this thought enter their view of reality. Of course Jesus was sent by God to save the nation Israel from its enemies. Of course he could not die. Peter had out-and-out rebuked Jesus for even suggesting it.

By this time he had also revealed—to a mixed response—that he was in fact the Messiah, the "Son of David." He had made the triumphal entry into Jerusalem. Peter had declared Jesus to be the Christ. At some level, most of the disciples saw him as the Messiah. Yet when the woman anointed his head, as would be appropriate for a king or a messiah, no one recognized the significance of her act. They rebuked her, harping on how much money she was throwing away.

Unlike the men, this woman knew who Jesus was. She had heard what Jesus had been saying. Perhaps she expected him to die at any moment, or perhaps she wanted to honor him as her messiah. Whatever the case, *she knew.* And she acted upon her knowledge.

Not only did she hear Jesus, but she heard her own deep wisdom confirming that what he said was the truth. Convinced he was on his way to death, she began, ceremonially at least, the process of tending his body. Awed at the presence of her king and messiah, and despite the men's opinions and their sharp rebuke, she broke open the flask and spilled precious ointment over his head. She respected her capacity to comprehend mystery, and she acted on it.

Because she had the courage to heed that spiritual wisdom, she was able to express to Jesus a most profound love. We can only imagine what it meant to Jesus that, finally, someone believed him, heard him, and was willing to walk alongside him, as much as possible, all the way to his tomb; or that a woman would risk such a negative reaction to declare him king while so many others still questioned and doubted him.

You and I love God, express friendship to the Divine, when we attend to the wisdom that God gives us. We dare move on a hunch. We follow our heart even if people call us crazy for it. We act in the absence of proof, and in so doing we make it possible for God to accomplish what God longs to accomplish.

Because we are willing to heed our wisdom, we are able to truly participate with God. We understand that portions of our life's path lie in the realm of the unknowable; thus our very obedience must reside at times in a cloud of mystery. But we're not so concerned about that. We know that what is ultimately important is that we hear God and follow God's voice.

———————————————————

As a novelist, I sometimes write
what I have not yet learned;
my Jungian friend says I should be grateful
I was born now and not in the age
of the witch trials. My mother sometimes
dreams things before they happen.
My father's mother received a vision,
decades ago, about what she was to do
with her life. My sister is not welcome
around unscrupulous men, because
she can read them like open books.
And once, when my husband was
engulfed in excruciating darkness,
I beheld, with no warning at all,
infinite circles of angels surrounding

Here in the Room

How would you describe the spiritual wisdom in your life?

What have you learned specifically from women and not from men? What kinds of information do you expect to receive from women, and why?

Are there spiritual practices (forms of prayer, meditation, work with the body) that you would use if you had permission to do so—from the church, or teachers, or your personal background of faith? If so, what are they, and why do you think you are drawn to them?

Have you experienced any spiritual hunches lately? If so, what are they? What would it take for you to act upon them?

In the coming week, allow yourself some quiet time every day to consider these questions:

> » God, are you trying to speak to me, and I'm not
>   hearing you?
> » Do I possess wisdom already that I am not
>   acknowledging?
> » Can I be open to whatever spiritual intuition the
>   Divine wants to impart to me?

CHAPTER 38

What difference does imagination make?

Where can I go from your spirit?
  Or where can I flee from your presence?
If I ascend to heaven, you are there;
  if I make my bed in Sheol, you are there.
If I take the wings of the morning
  and settle at the farthest limits of the sea,
even there your hand shall lead me,
  and your right hand shall hold me fast.
If I say, "Surely the darkness shall cover me,
  and the light around me become night,"
even the darkness is not dark to you;
  the night is as bright as the day,
  for darkness is as light to you.

Psalm 139:7–12

One of the loveliest books I've seen lately is *Moses: When Harriet Tubman Led Her People to Freedom*, a children's book written by Carole Boston Weatherford and illustrated by Kadir Nelson.[20] It is a fictional telling of Harriet's journey north and her subsequent career as a conductor on the Underground Railroad, the network of safe houses and secret routes that enabled slaves to escape to the North. According to Weatherford, Tubman made nineteen trips south, leading around three hundred slaves to freedom, including her own parents, without ever losing a passenger. Her success was accomplished through prayers, dreams, sharpened intuition, an intimate knowledge of nature, and the sheer resourcefulness to take on disguises, change routes, and solve problems as they materialized.

Harriet allowed her longing for freedom to open up her soul, and the result was an ability to imagine a different future and come up with ways to make it a reality. There is no one more imaginative than the person with a mission to which she is willing to dedicate her mind, strength, and spirit. Harriet believed that God had given her a mission, and her faith in God unleashed within her the powers of wisdom and imagination, not to mention endurance and courage.

We are born with imagination; it is one of our most crucial spiritual faculties. But the world stifles or nearly destroys it before we have reached adolescence. Corporate profits rely on people conforming to certain ways of doing things and to acceptable means of self-expression. Advertisers bombard young girls of age six or seven with images of what they should look like, thanks to clothing companies that create fashionable (and pricey) looks for babies, toddlers, children, and preteens. Before they are old enough to know what's happening, they are learning that to be acceptable a girl has to wear what someone else tells her is attractive.

School is not much better: our educational systems, obsessed with success that leads to funding, have eliminated much creativity and imagination from the classroom in order to teach specific sets of knowledge that will ensure high scores on standardized tests.

Our imagination is curtailed by faith communities as well. Most of us grow up with the concept that true worship looks like this but not like that. Prayer happens this way, and holy living involves A, B, and C. I've been around Pentecostals who can't get their minds around a prayer form such as the rosary, and Episcopalians who consider ecstatic prayer, such as speaking in tongues, to be verging on psychosis.

When we think beyond what is normal or possible, we are already in trouble. Harriet Tubman's husband refused to escape with her, even threatened to report her. How could one woman think she could escape from men with guns, horses, and bloodhounds? Was she out of her mind to set out on a journey of more than ninety miles with no resources but her own two feet and a lot of prayer?

Yet God's history with humanity is one long story of changing the status quo. A successful man named Abram is told to leave his security and go wandering with God. On several occasions a barren woman is told to get ready for the child that will be born to her. A young nation is given new sets of laws requiring mercy and justice—standards for looking after the orphan, widow, and alien—which move it far beyond the conventional modes of domination and empire building.

Then Jesus shows up, bringing along broader and deeper understandings of what it means to be faithful to God. Jesus breaks open the typical ideas concerning enemies, women, and the poor. Jesus demands that his disciples dare to see the world in a new way. And in the present day a handful of martyrs, such as Mahatma Gandhi and Martin Luther King Jr., imagine social change without the use of violence, and some forward-thinking business people realize that they can nourish local economies by setting up cooperatives among poor women, enabling them to get small loans so that they can set up businesses and help one another stay solvent.

We can name Dorothy Day and the Catholic Worker houses, Elizabeth Ann Seton and her school systems for marginalized children, Mother Teresa and her ministry to the destitute and dying, even people such as Princess Diana, who elevated world consciousness about the devastating impact of land mines on civilian communities and particularly the children in them. The only thing these women did was think a little further and imagine a little bigger.

If we are going to live as God's friends, we must prepare to do the same. When we join in what God is doing, the status quo won't be enough anymore. We must be willing to live along the borders where the old is transformed into the new. And we will have to learn how to welcome daydreams and wild thoughts rather than fear them.

How acquainted are you with your powers of imagination? How willing are you to envision a different life, or a different outcome to a situation? When was the last time you tried something new? Are you willing to say, "God, open me up and help me see the plans you have for my little part of the world"?

I was concerned, you see, about
the gifted artists who had no concept of
caring for their spiritual selves.
Also, I was tired of seeing faithful people too
frightened of their gifts to create lively art.
I suspected that spiritual life and creative life
were one and the same.
So I did a retreat sort of thing, just testing
the waters, but that weekend generated
even more longings and bigger ideas.
One thing led to another.
That was eight years and
how many workshops ago?
I'd never pictured myself in front of people—
I enjoy being behind the scenes—
but the room keeps filling up and here I am,
with books written, and people looking to
me. This is what happens when you give in
to a wild idea; this is what happens
when you ask, "What if . . .?"

Here in the Room ☕

What is the most imaginative thing you've ever done?

Who is the most imaginative person you know, and how would you describe that person's life and work?

Harriet Tubman, along with just about every other person who has done a great work or begun a holy enterprise, began simply with her own deep desire. For Harriet, that desire was to be free. What are your deep desires today? Or, what is your deep dissatisfaction?

Imagination is at the root of creation. What kind of world would you like to create? What kind of workplace? What kind of church? What kind of home?

During the next few days, generate as many ideas as you can about a particular desire or dissatisfaction. Just go crazy, and don't worry about how impractical the ideas are or how unqualified you may be to carry them out. Ask divine imagination to accompany you as you mull over these matters.

Pick something attractive you would like to create, and make steps this week to begin doing just that.

CHAPTER 39

How do you nurture God?

> May those who sow in tears
> reap with shouts of joy.
> Those who go out weeping,
> bearing the seed for sowing,
> shall come home with shouts of joy,
> carrying their sheaves.
>
> *Psalm 126:5–6*

I was unable to give birth to children, and I confess that this has been a continuing grief for me. I believe I've come to a healthy acceptance of this limitation. Moreover, my life is filled with good work to do and with more people than I have adequate time and energy to love well. Still, every now and then the reality will hit me with fresh pain: *You will live and die having never experienced pregnancy, birth, biological motherhood. You have missed one of life's most miraculous and fundamental experiences.*

Well, I think, *I mother people through my mentoring as an editor and as a workshop leader. In my own fashion I nurture stepsons and their families. I nurture a young girl whose mother died a few years ago. This motherhood impulse still finds good outlets, and, besides, I'm well into midlife now—this is an issue of diminishing importance.*

It was surprising, then, to see the metaphor of pregnancy emerge clearly when I spent extended time in prayer a few months ago. Here I considered that I'd let go of the whole idea, put it away with other topics that no longer held much personal meaning. But divine love brought it right back out again. The one thought that overtook nearly every other, as the retreat drew to an end, was that I am, right now, "pregnant with God."

Mary of Nazareth may have been in a class by herself, but I believe more and more that she was making a way for the rest of us. We are at every moment growing God in the privacy and loveliness of our own lives. We are nourishing God in our habits and prayers and daily acts of purpose and praise. And we keep giving birth to God, in our revelations and our brave words, in our hard work to make visions real. Mary was the first of many mothers. This was God's plan all along.

Our great privilege as women is that we have a physical, whole-self understanding of what it means for something completely new to form within us, and for us to wait and then labor to bring that life to birth. Even those of us who are not biological mothers have a knowledge of this. We sense life-bearing not only through our routine bodily pains and cycles but also through the memories of our mothers and grandmothers and through the stories of sisters and friends. This sensibility can assist us as we express our love to God through our capacity to be mother.

Please consider this: Within your lovely, spectacular self is a dark and quiet place—your womb. This is where holy wonders are taking shape. They form in you because *only your life* can nourish them. Your memories, your losses, your hungers, and your fantastic imaginings spin together the bones and sinews, the eyes and fingers of God, the real and living God. This is the manifestation of divine life that you, and only you, can bring into the world.

In our mothering capacity we express love to God when we nurture others. The world has always seen women as nourishers, because the young feed at our breasts. In fact, women have often borne the greater burden of tending others because that role seemed to fit us so well. Men, too, have capacity to nurture, but far too many men have neglected to develop that gift. Quite a few have instead relied on women to take care of them— first mother, then sister, then girlfriend or wife and, in old age, daughter. When societies allow men to ignore their abilities to nurture and to grow too dependent on others, all of us suffer from the imbalance. Still, that's no reason for women to neglect their nurturing gifts.

We nurture by transforming physical spaces into home, even if that home is a temporary location for a three-day retreat. We nurture by providing a safe emotional space in which others can heal and grow. We nurture by paying attention to the quality of life around us and insisting on change when necessary. We nurture through mentoring.

I am a feast-maker. I come from a long line of women feast-makers on both sides of the family. We derive joy from preparing meals for others—and others enjoy this, because we are good cooks! This impulse has posed a challenge for me over the years, because I didn't have a brood of children growing up around me, needing my feasts. Holidays were especially hard. We nearly always traveled to feast at a mother's home, or with siblings whose homes were more centrally located and better suited to accommodate multiple guests. So Jim and I created occasions for feasting—parties themed around Italian or Middle Eastern movies, or parties to celebrate a new book's publication or some other event. For a few people, our home has been a retreat—a good space away from their own apartment or neighborhood where they could relax, do work if necessary, and be fed by us.

A woman once called out to Jesus, "Blessed is the womb that bore you and the breasts that nursed you!" But Jesus said, "Blessed rather are those who hear the word of God and obey it!"[21] One thing I've always appreciated about Jesus is his lack of sentimentality. In this one statement he gets past biology and misplaced zeal to say, "Every one of us has work to do in this world." You and I may nurse children, or not. We may even nurse children who grow up to be great heroes of the faith. But our mothering gifts extend far beyond that role.

If you haven't already, then it's high time you asked yourself: What are my gifts for nurturing God's life in the world? In what way is God growing in the womb that is my life?

I grow you, sweet Jesus, within myself.
I carry you everywhere I go.
Some days I sing songs for you or
tell the stories you need to know.
Over you I hover, all around you
I whisper wonders and blessings.
You form in delicate peace within
the circle of my womb-love,
are carried upon my hips, my two legs.
I enclose you in my desiring yet empty
arms; I pulse into you every holy wisdom
from the fierce love-beat of my tender
and tenuous heart.
Around this embryo of Divine-ness,
egg of very substance,
has my womb formed and stretched.
I have ached and bled,
have rocked myself in the corner, afraid.
I have wondered, with many tears,
what love will look like when it's born,
and I have laughed with confounding joy
to consider the great tearing open to come,
the shock, the bright immensity
of life brought forth.

Here in the Room

Draw a picture of your womb—that is, draw a womb-shape and then draw within it images, or write words and phrases, that represent the life you are bringing forth right now. I suggest that you do this assignment quickly and then set it aside for a day or two, praying over those words and images, asking God to help you see clearly the nurturing gifts and opportunities that are present to you.

With the benefit of prayer and some time to ponder, go back to your womb picture and either revise it or draw a fresh version of it. Then, when you are ready, share it with a friend. Do this with the openness to receive that friend's response to what you've drawn. It's very likely that your friend will have some things to add to the picture.

CHAPTER 40

Why is passion important?

As a deer longs for flowing streams,
  so my soul longs for you, O God.
My soul thirsts for God,
  for the living God.
When shall I come and behold
  the face of God?
My tears have been my food
  day and night,
while people say to me continually,
  "Where is your God?"

Psalm 42:1–3

In the film *Steel Magnolias*, Sally Field plays a mother whose twenty-something daughter dies of kidney failure. After the funeral, the mother is talking with her circle of women friends, describing what it was like to sit with her daughter while she died. The young woman's husband couldn't bear to stay, and neither could her father or brothers. So this mother had sat there alone while her child died. "I realize, as a woman, how lucky I am. I was there when that wonderful creature drifted into my life, and I was there when she drifted out. It was the most precious moment of my life," she says.

I'm sure there are good dictionary definitions of passion, but I prefer this one: Passion is the love by which we stay the course, no matter what. Passion keeps us at the bedside of the sick and dying. Passion keeps loving and forgiving when life is hard and people stumble. In the way that mature love never fails, as stated in 1 Corinthians 13, passion stays.

We could point to Mary the mother of Jesus to represent a woman's passionate love. But another Mary shows up repeatedly in the scenes of Jesus' life. All we really know of her from the Gospels is that she, too, was named Mary, known as Mary of Magdala, and that Jesus had cast seven demons out of her. Evidently she followed him from that point on. She was one of several women who traveled with Jesus and the twelve disciples, providing for them out of their own means. We can imagine this group of women going to the market in whatever town Jesus was ministering, buying food and other supplies, and making sure Jesus and his inner circle were fed. We can imagine them dealing with the women and children who came to Jesus, organizing and encouraging. I suspect that whenever a person stood waiting to see Jesus, one of these women was nearby, engaging them in conversation, getting them a drink of water, just being there.

I can't picture Mary of Magdala being quiet and reserved because, well, Jesus had freed her from the oppression/possession of seven demons. However you want to think of her deliverance, she was definitely a woman restored, reborn, with a story to tell and with enthusiastic love for the God who had given her life back to her. I think she was probably a bundle of holy energy, working the crowd in her own way, witnessing to the reality of transformation. I'll bet she had no problem looking anyone in the eye and saying, "God loves you more than you could ever love yourself." I'll bet she said that a lot, to anyone who would listen.

She was one of a handful of people who followed Jesus all the way to the cross. She watched him die. I believe she was right there with his mother, not leaving her side for a moment. I imagine that Jesus' death nearly finished her off because Jesus represented everything to her: life, peace of mind, a future, love, wholeness.

And she was one of the women who, at early dawn, dared go to the tomb of Jesus the executed criminal, to talk someone into rolling the stone from the entrance so that they could properly anoint his mutilated body and bury it, finally, with peace and gentleness. But there was no body to anoint and weep over.

Imagine how you would feel if the funeral home misplaced the body of your brother or father or husband. Imagine all the women who have had no body to tend, such as the hundreds and thousands in El Salvador or Uganda whose loved ones were simply "disappeared" or were so mangled there were only unidentifiable pieces left. Imagine all the women through history who have collected the blood-soaked dirt because that was all that remained after the enemies had gone and the fires and wild animals had finished off the dead. Included in the story of Jesus are many, many other stories of death and the passionate love that stays right there, in the face of annihilation and unspeakable grief.

> But Mary [Magdalene] stood weeping outside the tomb. As she wept, she bent over to look into the tomb; and she saw two angels in white, sitting where the body of Jesus had been lying, one at the head and the other at the feet. They said to her, "Woman, why are you weeping?" She said to them, "They have taken away my Lord, and I do not know where they have laid him." When she had said this, she turned around and saw Jesus standing there, but she did not know that it was Jesus. Jesus said to her, "Woman, why are you weeping? Whom are you looking for?" Supposing him to be the gardener, she said to him, "Sir, if you have carried him away, tell me where you have laid him, and I will take him away."
>
> —John 20:11–15

Please pause now and imagine this woman, a nobody to anyone who mattered, deciding on the spot that she will, all on her own, take charge of a dead body. What she thought she could do is anybody's guess. But Mary of Magdala was passionate to the core. She would stay with Jesus to the brutal end.

And when the supposed gardener revealed that he was Jesus, when he said her name, "Mary," and she recognized him, we know that she reached to embrace him, because he had to tell her not to cling to him. She did not respond with fear or doubt ("So, if you're really Jesus, let's see those scars"). No, she followed her passion and cast aside confusion and logical dissonance. All that mattered was that Jesus was there, and she was prepared to do anything for him. He told her to go tell the others, and that's what she did.

> *Now after he rose early on the first day of the week, he appeared first to Mary Magdalene, from whom he had cast out seven demons. She went out and told those who had been with him, while they were mourning and weeping. But when they heard that he was alive and had been seen by her, they would not believe it.*
>
> —*Mark 16:9–11*

Their doubts probably frustrated Mary, but they didn't cause so much as a moment's hesitation in this woman's continuing journey of faith.

When we love truly, the passion takes shape and becomes real with each event, each challenge, each task. Our passion is expressed in the love that keeps going and going.

It's not that I'm particularly strong
or courageous. I get tired too quickly and
need much assurance and sometimes
I eat more chocolate than is healthy.
Don't call me heroic, for heaven's sake.
But I'm invested, quite invested in the people
of my life, also the neighborhood I live in,
and the country I call home,
and the institutions that claim to exist
for my benefit. I feel parts and pieces
of myself tangled, woven into all
the living things, down to the bright
little zinnias that flourish in a front yard
just south of here. When you're that
connected to the specifics of the world,
it's possible to fight hopeless battles,
to stand rooted to the spot where
blood is spilled. Passion is simply love
grown deep into a stony landscape.

Here in the Room ☕——————

This week, invite into the Room two or three friends. Have lunch or coffee together when you have time to be relaxed. Then, one by one, each of you tell a story about the most passionate person you know personally.

Finish the following statement. If necessary, allow it to grow into a little story: "One day, passion appeared in my life, and this is what happened . . ."

Dwell a little longer . . .

In working through this book, you have spent significant time here in the Room with God. Listed below are a few suggestions for how to process what this has been like for you. Try one or more as you feel so inclined.

Create a page of faces. You can draw them or cut them out of magazines or download them from the Internet. These faces have come to represent God to you. Next to each face you might write a short paragraph or poem or just a phrase that explains how you connect this face to the Divine.

Go through the Table of Contents and pick one chapter out of each of the eight parts of the book. These are the chapters that spoke to you most powerfully. Review them and go back to what you did in the Here in the Room sections.

Write a story of your journey through the book. Or write a story of your journey through a specific chapter or section.

Here are the titles of the eight parts of the book. Beside each word, write a statement that represents your response to this aspect of friendship with God.

Beginning

Hesitation

Awareness

Resistance

Conversation

Attention

Engagement

Love

Write a letter to God, your friend. Say whatever you need to say, in whatever way you need to say it.

If you want to be a little daring . . .

Write God's letter to you, friend of the Divine.

How to use this book with small groups

Agroup process creates its own dynamic, and so working through materials as a group will be a different experience from doing it alone. I suggest a few guidelines.

Agree on confidentiality. The subject matter in *Days of Deepening Friendship* is quite personal, and group members must agree that everything shared in the group will be kept in confidence.

Choose who will lead, and how. Perhaps one of your members is experienced in leading group work and discussion. If so, the group may ask her to lead through the entire process. If the group decides that people can take turns leading, it would be best to have a standard format to follow, so that each person doesn't have to invent one.

Decide which portions of the work will be done as a group. There's enough material in this book to keep a group going for months. I suggest that your group focus on only certain aspects of each chapter and leave the rest for people to do on their own. Perhaps at the end of each meeting, the group can decide which portions they'll focus on for next time. This is particularly important when it comes to the Here in The Room sections, which generally offer multiple options for activity and reflection.

Identify what additional materials and/or activities might be added. As the group works with the material, it's possible that particular issues will emerge as being more important than others. If this happens, you might need to rethink how to use the time. For instance, the chapters on prayer might lead to more extensive work in this area, involving more time with Scripture or other books or more time to pray as a group, if that's what you decide to do.

Stay away from arguments. The purpose of *Days of Deepening Friendship* is to explore what it means to be friends with God. Avoid wrangling over church teaching or controversy, which will merely disrupt the better work at hand.

Above all, choose love and acceptance. Make friendship among yourselves a goal of these meetings. You will be sharing from your personal experience and telling some of your own stories. Be kind to one another. Practice expressing divine love throughout your discussions.

Locate help if you need it. If, in the context of this work together, it becomes clear that a group member is in crisis, be proactive in finding additional help as necessary. For instance, one of you may discover that what you thought was desolation is really severe depression. The appropriate response is to find a professional to help deal with that.

If this is a good experience for you, spread the word! After having worked through *Days of Deepening Friendship*, you may be well qualified to help a new group embark on that journey.

Acknowledgments

This is the book that I kept hoping would cross my editorial desk at Loyola Press. When nobody wrote that book, I decided to write it myself. Thanks to a supportive team, I was able to do that in a relatively short time. Many thanks to my Loyola colleagues, especially Tom McGrath, Jim Campbell, and Terry Locke, whose early enthusiasm helped me stay the course.

Many wise women have shaped my life, writers such as Madeleine L'Engle and Emilie Griffin, publishing colleagues such as Lynn Vanderzalm and Phyllis Tickle, and soul friends such as Lil Copan and Cindy Crosby. (Each of these categories includes numerous others, but in trying to be comprehensive I would neglect someone, so I will leave it at this.) LaVonne Neff edited this book and provided exactly the touch it needed, so I am indebted to her now not only for her many years of friendship but for her analytic and intuitive wisdom as well. Rebecca Johnson, who did the copyedit, is on my list of Most Admired Women simply for who she is but also for adding her skills to this work.

I thank the many pastors, teachers, and church members who have walked alongside as I have learned to pay attention to

God's love in my life. Especially important to the earlier years were Debbie, Mary, Trudy, Barbara, Dave, and Brother James. I'm grateful to the various people who informed the faith of my college days, and to the outstanding men and women I served with in Jordan years ago.

I am one of the most fortunate women on earth because I was loved early in life by women who had longstanding friendships with the Divine. I name Virginia Bevins and Lorraine Lee, grandmothers with good sense who knew how to pray and who had well-honed nonsense detectors in matters of faith and life in general. They are enjoying their friendship with God up close now, having passed this world's confines. I name my mother, Virginia Hampton, who has lived her faith and love for more than seventy years and who has taught me how to embrace my life and enjoy the miracle of ordinary moments. I name my sisters, Valinda and Valerie, who know how to weather storms, speak the truth, and love well while laughing loudly. I name Vinita Jones, the Pentecostal preacher/pastor for whom I was named. I have never met another human being so capable of walking into a room and by a word or a smile convincing you that you are the absolute focus of God's passionate love. Vinita died just a few years ago, and I'm beginning to suspect that she has passed along some sort of mantle to me, a job to do in this world that involves introducing others to the greatest Friend of all.

Notes

1. Emilie Griffin, *Clinging: The Experience of Prayer* (Wichita, KS: Eighth Day Books, 2003), 1.

2. St. Teresa of Ávila, *The Way of Perfection*, ch. 28, tr. E. Allison Peers, in *Complete Works of St. Teresa*, vol 2 (New York: Sheed & Ward, 1972), p. 114–15, quoted in *The Lion Christian Meditation Collection* compiled by Hannah Ward and Jennifer Wild (Oxford, England: Lion Publishing, 1998), 336–37.

3. Kerry Egan, *Fumbling: A Pilgrimage Tale of Love, Grief, and Spiritual Renewal on the Camino de Santiago* (New York: Doubleday, 2004), 81.

4. Concepción Cabrera de Armida, *Before the Altar*, trans. by Luisa Icaza de Medina Mora, intro by Most Reverend Donald W. Montrose (Mexico: Ediciones Cimiento, A.C., 1915, 1988), quoted in *Prayers of the Women Mystics* ed. by Ronda De Sola Chervin (Ann Arbor, MI: Servant Publications, 1992), 191.

5. Galatians 5:22–23.

6. Mechtild of Magdeburg, "True Sorrow," from *The Soul Afire: Revelations of the Mystics* (New York: Pantheon Books, 1944), 113, quoted in *Silent Voices, Sacred Lives: Women's Readings for*

the Liturgical Year, by Barbara Bowe, et al. (New York: Paulist Press, 1992), 76.

7. Madeleine L'Engle, *Bright Evening Star: Mystery of the Incarnation* (Colorado Springs, CO: Waterbrook Press, 1997), 21.

8. Sybil MacBeth, *Praying in Color: Drawing a New Path to God* (Brewster, MA: Paraclete Press, 2007).

9. Luke 2:51.

10. Acts 13:1–3.

11. Evelyn Underhill, *Practical Mysticism* (New York: E. P. Dutton & Company, 1915, accessed through Christian Classics Ethereal Library online edition, 2007), 11.

12. *The Spiritual Exercises of Saint Ignatius,* translation and commentary by George E. Ganss (St. Louis: Institute of Jesuit Sources, 1992), 122.

13. Ibid.

14. Katherine Dyckman, Mary Garvin, and Elizabeth Liebert, *The Spiritual Exercises Reclaimed: Uncovering Liberating Possibilities for Women* (New York: Paulist Press, 2001), 125–26.

15. Vinita Hampton Wright, *The Soul Tells a Story: Engaging Creativity with Spirituality in the Writing Life* (Downers Grove, IL: InterVarsity Press, 2005).

16. Ephesians 4:11–13.

17. I've read various books on the Spiritual Exercises and Ignatian spirituality, but one book that summarizes well the aspects of good discernment is Chris Lowney's *Heroic Living: Discover Your Purpose and Change the World* (Loyola Press, 2009), chapter 8.

18. Suzanna Wesley, quoted in *2000 Years of Prayer*, comp. Michael Counsell (Harrisburg, PA: Morehouse Publishing, 1999), 312.

19. Leila Ahmed, *A Border Passage: From Cairo to America—A Woman's Journey* (New York: Farrar, Straus and Giroux, 1999). See the full discussion on pages 120–131.

20. *Moses: When Harriet Tubman Led Her People to Freedom*, written by Carole Boston Weatherford, illustrated by Kadir Nelson (New York: Hyperion Books for Children, 2006).

21. Luke 11:27–28.

About the Author

VINITA HAMPTON WRIGHT has been a book editor for nearly two decades and a retreat/workshop leader for eight years. Her most recent novel, *Dwelling Places,* won the Christianity Today award for Best Fiction of 2007. Her nonfiction books include *The Soul Tells a Story: Engaging Creativity with Spirituality in the Writing Life*; *A Catalogue of Angels*; *The St. Thérèse of Lisieux Prayer Book*; and *Simple Acts of Moving Forward: 60 Suggestions for Getting Unstuck.* Ms. Wright lives in Chicago with her husband, the photographer Jim Wright.

You Are Invited

If you would like to hear about and participate in online workshops conducted by Vinita Wright that would continue the experience you've been enjoying with *Days of Deepening Friendship*, sign up at **www.loyolapress.com/vinita-retreats.htm**. Loyola Press will be glad to send you notices as those online experiences are scheduled.